CHANGE OF KEY

CHANGE OF KEY

Models for Festival Worship

Frederick W. Kemper

Publishing House
St. Louis

This book is dedicated
to the sinners and saints of
Calvary Lutheran Congregation

Unless otherwise stated, the Bible quotations in this publication are from the Revised Standard Version of the Bible, copyrighted 1946, 1952, © 1971, 1973 by the Division of Christian Education of the National Council of the Churches of Christ in the U.S.A., and used by permission.

References marked Phillips are reprinted with permission of Macmillan Publishing Co., Inc., from *The New Testament in Modern English* by J. B. Phillips, Revised Edition © J. B. Phillips 1958, 1960, 1972.

Excerpts from *The Jerusalem Bible*, copyright © 1966 by Darton, Longman & Todd, Ltd. and Doubleday & Company, Inc. Used by permission of the publisher.

Quotations from *The New English Bible,* © The Delegates of the Oxford University Press and The Syndics of the Cambridge University Press, 1961, 1970, reprinted by permisson.

Concordia Publishing House, St. Louis, Missouri
Copyright © 1977 Concordia Publishing House

MANUFACTURED IN THE UNITED STATES OF AMERICA

Library of Congress Cataloging in Publication Data

Kemper, Frederick W
    A change of key.

    1. Lutheran Church. Liturgy and ritual.
2. Liturgies—Lutheran Church. I. Title.
BX8067.A3K45   264'.04'1   77-21775
ISBN 0-570-03761-1

CONTENTS

FOREWORD

This book of worship services is exceedingly presumptuous. Please know that I have no quarrel with any committee working on liturgy for the church. They are seeking a more permanent solution to the terribly perplexing problem of weekly worship. These suggestions of mine are as expendable as banners, as one-time as an ice cream cone.

Yet I dare to be presumptuous because there seems a need for variety in liturgy and too few channels filling that need. Many pastors would like to do something different in worship, but the mechanics and resources elude them. These sampling services will hopefully help them find a way to worship differently.

My interest in worship began in the youth camps and schools of another year when I planned many morning devotions and campfire vespers. Those little services had to be held together with one stout thread or another. The ideas developed in those wonderful camp years were easily enough translated and amplified into stepping stones for new worship services for the adult community. Developing such orders as are included in this book has been one of the exciting facets of my ministry.

Who knows where these expressions of liturgy will go and what they will accomplish? Since they are now in your hands, I hope you will find something you can use among them, and so praise God in a new key.

These are service models. They are a record of services that have actually been used and which the users of this book may adapt to their own needs and resources. For example, anthems are listed in the places where they may appear, but they may be replaced with similar suitable anthems; for the hymns listed substitute hymns on the same theme can be selected.

Incidentally, I am very grateful to Concordia Publishing House for publishing them. They make it possible for me to share them with you, which is what our Lord's parable of the talents is all about.

F. W. K.

CHANGE OF KEY

Sing a New Song
The Mass
Doing Liturgy

Sing a New Song

"Going to church is like going to the theater," wrote the blooming young Christian in an essay on worship. "The chancel is the stage, the pastor is the actor, and the congregation is the audience."

His teacher gave him an *A* on his grammar, but wrote a note to the pupil to help him understand how wrong he was in his metaphor. "Really," the teacher wrote, "the congregation is the actor and God is the audience. The pastor is the prompter."

"Wrong, too," says the theologian and the liturgist to the teacher. "The actor in a church service is God. The people are the responders. The role of the pastor or officiant is to enable the power and love of God to reach and to affect the responders."

By way of definition, worship is "man's response to God." The definition can be a lot more complicated, but "man's response to God" suggests enough activity to work out a vast array of worship services or liturgies, without violating the "role" of God or the "role" of the worshiping congregation.

Worship postulates God. As a word, it assumes that God exists and is known by the worshiper. It assumes, too, that God comes to man directly or "by way of," effecting His purposes in responsive people. Anyone who presumes to arrange worship services must not only be aware of how and why God works, but why and how and what responses happen among the members of the congregation.

The postulate is that God has always existed. When the church fathers wondered how it was before God disclosed Himself at creation, they imagined Him in a deep and brooding silence, which they called the *Mysterium Stupendum* (with variations including *Mysterium Maiestas* and *Fascinans*). It was a gracious act of God that He allowed Himself to be known by His creatures, visible and invisible.

They could respond to Him in praise and thanksgiving. The angelic myriads sang their "Holy, holy, holy" hymns. Adam and Eve, in amazing familiarity, walked the garden paths with Him, yet the God/man relationship was not abused.

At the Fall God came in judgment. In the promise of Christ, God came in mercy. He was the "actor" in the establishment of the covenants between Himself and His people. He was the actor in the arrival of the prophets with their messages of doom and hope. He was the actor in the promise to Abraham and the fulfillment of that promise in the advent of His Son. He was the actor through the person of Christ by whom the world was redeemed. He initiated and initiates reconciliation. He is posed even now between the Resurrection and the trumpets of the denouement. Into eternity, He will control the affairs of glory.

It is through the mission and the purpose of the Holy Spirit that He acts, especially and overtly since Pentecost. It is the work of the Spirit to "call, gather, enlighten, and sanctify" each Christian and the whole Christian church on earth, as Martin Luther pointed out in his explanation to the early church's credal statements about Him. Through the Word, written, preached, in the mouth of the brother, the Holy Spirit calls and keeps men in the saving faith. Through the sacraments He brings forgiveness and sustains the faith. "So faith comes from what is heard, and what is heard comes by the preaching of Christ" (Rom. 10:17). ". . . no one can say 'Jesus is Lord' except by the Holy Spirit" (1 Cor. 12:3).

To make worship happen, assuming that the definition and the third revision of the essay are correct, God, the holy and blessed Trinity, must be the starting point. His presence must be *a priori* supposed. His gracious acts must be recounted; His abiding power inherent in the Word must be accepted.

Worship, when it happens, sometimes oozes, sometimes explodes in a variety of ways within the "worship hour." Since the only offering people can bring to God is praise and thanksgiving, praise and thanksgiving are, or ought to be, the first great explosion. "We have something to whoop and holler about," explained a Christian from a "whoop and holler" church. "We say 'Alleluia' a lot in our church," rejoined a Christian from a liturgical persuasion. Both are acceptable ways for creatures to praise their Creator, for sinners to thank their redeeming Lord, and for citizens to adore their gracious King.

Prayer, a most acceptable activity that acknowledges the dominion of God and opens the soul to His Word and promises, is response. Amens are affirmations to God's mighty deeds. The great creeds are "stand up and be counted" words, the pledge of loyalty of liege to Lord. Listening to the Word, hearing the Word, from Scripture or from the mouth of the brother, calls for the death of the "Old Adam in us," assures us of God's might and power, His grace and benevolence, or becomes marching orders to the "battle station" to which assignment has been made to live out the Christian life. Then, sometimes, a warm glow brought on by the rediscovery of God's love, or an uncontrollable wonder brought on by God's majesty, or an irresistible excitement occasioned by a new insight, happens. Worship is going on! When the struggle of sin and guilt ceases, a decision is made, a new direction is determined, a burden is lightened, worship is going on.

Worship at its best begins when the worship hour is over. Having been with God in the midst of the community, the worshiper is put to the test of his "audience with the King" in the minute-to-minute, day-to-day stuff of living. How will he or she live in the family—having been with God? How will the "enemy" be treated? What will be said to the nasty neighbor or the petulant boss? What thoughts will be retained and what words will escape? Soon, too soon, the Old Adam asserts itself. The bruises come. Prayers and repentance and forgiveness and soaking up a little love are in order again. Back to sanctuary, back to the community, back to the healing presence of God, they come.

The Mass

The church developed her liturgies, or orders of worship, gradually. Forms of the Old Testament worship carried over into New Testament times. As the church matured, she developed forms of her own. It is quite possible to demonstrate liturgical remnants from the early generations of the Christians, even in Scripture. As the centuries unrolled, liturgies developed and crystallized. First among them was the work of the Eastern Church. The Roman Rites grew out of the orders and forms developed in the West. It is on these forms that the medieval Mass form was based.

Through her liturgies the church expressed herself in customs, rite, form, definiteness. Much survived the testing of time, much did not. Yet always the church was expressing herself, her doctrine, her authority, her sham, by what she did in her worship hours. For a thousand years the church had maintained the form of the Mass of the medieval church. True, Calvin elected not to use it, but Luther adjusted it to his reform principles, and Cranmer reworked it to suit the purposes of the new English Church. The Mass is exciting, as one follows it through the death and resurrection of Christ and realizes that Christ is present in the elements.

The medieval church used symbols to convey the message of the Gospel to her people. In the mass every detail had its significance. The following sentences of Gulielmus Durandus in *Rationale*, quoted by Emile Male in the introduction to *The Gothic Image*, illustrate the degree to which symbolism was carried in the Middle Ages. At the same time they offer insight into the Roman Rite or the revised masses of many Protestants.

The ceremony begins with the *Introit*, that solemn chant which expresses the waiting of patriarchs and prophets. The choir of clergy is the very choir of the saints of the Ancient Law who sigh for the coming of the Messiah whom they will never see. The bishop then enters, appearing as the living type of Christ, and his arrival symbolises the coming of the Saviour awaited by the nations. Before him at great festivals are carried seven lights to recall the seven gifts of the Spirit which rested upon the head of the Son of God, according to the word of the prophet. He advances under a triumphal canopy whose four bearers may be compared to the four evangelists. To right and left of him walk acolytes, typifying Moses and Elias, who were seen on Mount Tabor on either side of the transfigured Lord. They teach men that the authority of both the Law and the Prophets was embodied in Christ. The bishop seats himself on his throne and is silent, appearing to take no share in the first part of the ceremony. His attitude contains a lesson, for by his silence he recalls that the first years of the life of Jesus were passed in obscurity and meditation. The sub-deacon, however, goes to the desk, and turning to the right, he reads the Epistle aloud. Here we catch a glimpse of the first act in the drama of Redemption, for the reading of the Epistle typifies the preaching of John the Baptist in the desert. He speaks before the Saviour has begun His mission, but he speaks to the Jews alone, and the sub-deacon—type of the Forerunner—turns to the north, the side of the Old Law. The reading ended, he bows to the bishop as John the Baptist abased himself before his Master.*

A little amplification of the Mass might be in order. The French government worked out a solar furnace in which the rays of the sun

* From *The Gothic Image: Religious Art in the Thirteenth Century* by Emile Male, translated by Dora Nussy. Published in the United States by E. P. Dutton, and reprinted with their permission.

are caught by an adjustable mirror; from which they are focused on a parabolic reflector, intensifying and reflecting them to a concave mirror. Once again they are intensified. At the focal point the furnace temperature reaches 9,000° F., more than half the heat of the surface of the sun. The church, determining her Order for worshiping God, concentrated the redeeming history of God, which the Spirit had gathered into the Holy Scripture, and focused it in her liturgy. At the center focus is Jesus Christ. To be aware of the unfolding history in the Mass is to be aware that Christ is at the center of it. In the Sanctus, the Palm Sunday procession passes by—and the worshiper is part of it. In the Consecration he sits with the disciples at the paschal feast and is present at the presentation of the new covenant. In the Agnus Dei he weeps again for the dying Christ. His mind and heart fill with the moment of the Passover sacrifice. But then it is Easter. Christ comes to the worshiper in the bread and wine. He is alive! He is present! Easter is now! Easter is here! The song of Simeon is the pledge of allegiance of Christ's people. "We have seen You! Now let us go out and die for You!"

The Mass of the Middle Ages adapted into the contemporary scene has not lost its validity or its power. It provides for every worshiper a vision of Christ. The sermon may not speak to him; the lessons may not apply to him; the choir may not be to his liking, but through the story of the Mass Christ emerges to quietly, forcefully, put His arm around the worshiper that he may be strong again. He has not been allowed to forget his Christ. He has had an encounter with God. He has been involved with his Redeemer, the risen and reigning Lord.

Doing Liturgy

Liturgy has come to mean "the order of worship" to most people. Its roots as a word go back into ancient soil, where it meant voluntary service to the government. From there it was an easy step to "voluntary service to God." The step from service as ministry to service as "order of worship" is also short. The final step being taken by many Christians presently is back closer to liturgy's first Christianized meaning of voluntary service to the Lord. In this book, however, "liturgy" is used to denote the worship service format.

Requirements for Liturgy

Through the long years of her history, the church has developed parts and pieces which seem necessary to the development of good liturgy. Hymns, invocations, confessions and absolution, Scripture readings, affirmations of faith, meditations, sermons, prayers, benedictions—all have a place in liturgical orders. Today even "secular" material may on occasion find its way into liturgical forms quite acceptably. Traditionally, the church has been fairly rigid in its use of forms for worship. The atmosphere in these now decades has become freer, as new and contemporary forms are being offered by the liturgical committees of the church and as individuals seek to express their needs in their own way.

There is in the church a new awareness of all the senses. Consequently, contemporary worship spaces are being devised to allow new freedom of movement and new visual excitement. Color, in appointments, in vestments, and in the building itself, has come into its own. The sounds are different, from atonal music to guitars. The postures of worship have acquired new freedoms. It is possible now to face your fellow worshiper, look at him, the while confessing faith in the Trinity in the words of the Apostles' Creed, or to move about for the kiss of peace, and heaven forbid! to smile, to laugh, and to applaud.

Should a pastor want to write a liturgy, and certainly the urge descends at times on most pastors, he has at his disposal his own talents in the area, a plethora of material gathered for just such a purpose, the host of hymns produced by the centuries, all of Scripture, as well as, on occasion, material from profane sources. A liturgy doesn't just happen, however. It is born of prayer, of experience, of discipline, of a knowledge of how the Holy Spirit works, and of careful structuring. The would-be liturgist is circumscribed by his community's resources, the ability of the organist, the availability of trumpets, the artistic talent, the educational level of his people, any of which can be asset or detriment.

Composing a Liturgy

To be acceptable a liturgy ought to "go somewhere." That means the liturgist cannot put together a series of religious particles or a "cute" idea and develop a respectable or acceptable liturgy. The liturgy must develop step by step, proceeding through hymns and lessons, prayers and responses, sermon and Sacrament to its purpose, to a climax and a conclusion. The services in this book are meant to demonstrate such composition. In the service for Good Friday the denouement falls in a crescendo and silence at the terror-filled words from the cross, "My God! My God! Why hast Thou forsaken Me?" In the Christmas morning service the climax falls on the hymn before the Benediction, "Now let all the heavens adore Thee." Notice that in the Mass, the ultimate conclusion is in the distribution of the elements, when the risen, present, living Christ comes to each worshiper. It may happen that the service begins with a majestic processional. What follows could easily be anticlimactic. If the whole service has been kept in mind, an even more exciting moment will be planned somewhere in the service.

Resources for Liturgy

The first great resource for liturgy is the church's wellspring, the Bible. Here the mighty acts of God in the covenants, in Jesus Christ, in the sacraments, or any of the many concepts that thread through Scripture, beg for development. Why couldn't the life-death-life motif, noticeable especially in Romans 6, but inherent in the Red Sea experience, in Confession, and in man's total life cycle as well, be developed into an exciting service for Holy Saturday, or a Baptism service? Or why not develop a liturgy on the kingdom of God motif which Jesus came to proclaim? Or the Law-Gospel-love tensions which are so basic to the Christian faith.

Church tradition offers another source for service development. The theme of the church for the dark and dreary season of the year was "Light"; the coming of longer and sunnier days in spring saw "life" as theme. Then why shouldn't Christmas through Epiphany capitalize on "light" and Easter through Pentecost celebrate "Life"? The church commemorated the passion of Jesus on Palm Sunday. Then why shouldn't a Palm Sunday liturgy move relentlessly from Bethany to the cross, passing the shouting people on the way? A little research on the traditional antiphons and responses, prayers, and Scripture readings will open new patterns.

Lutherans, Romans, Episcopalians, and others are involved in liturgies of all shapes and forms. Keeping a little abreast of the very fluid current scene offers much resource material. Some services can be adapted and adopted for variety. Many compilations of invocations, prayers, litanies, confessions, etc., are available. Careful picking and choosing from compilations for just the proper paragraph is certainly permissible.

Outside sources are many, but should be used with discretion. A Tre Ore service might be enhanced with pieces of poetry. A Thanksgiving service can certainly borrow from the notes and papers of the people of the past who braved this new land that God had given them. The playwrights and novelists can become the world speaking to the church. Would it be so wrong to read a little of Rolf Hochhuth's *The Deputy* or the name chapter of Henryk Sienkiewicz' *Quo Vadis?* or the Christmas sermon of Becket in T. S. Eliot's *Murder in the Cathedral?* The use of such sources must by their nature be most carefully chosen to cohere and advance the thesis of the liturgy or the message for the day.

The Congregation

Once the service has been written, the congregation must be considered. It is important that introductory notes be made, either orally or in the worship folder. It is equally important that a minimum of book shuffling be built into the liturgy. Actually, it is best if the whole service—hymns, psalms, responsive readings, or whatever the congregation may be doing—be in hand in printed form. The service moves with measured sweep and far better comprehension when the whole liturgy is available to those who are living it.

A printed service allows for freedom for the liturgist. He can pick and choose stanzas of hymns, intersperse them with readings, and get into them quickly in the worship hour if they are printed. If the hymns are printed without melody line, the tune should be familiar to the congregation. Directions for posturing can be inserted, eliminating hand signals. Explanations and interpretations for the choice of material can be included in parenthetical printed remarks. It might even be desirable at a narrative Communion to print out the narrative material for later review.

The Participants

It is most unfair to draw someone into service at the last moment and say, "Here, do this." From acolytes to trumpet soloists, each participant is entitled to advance warning, and a good understanding of his or her place and purpose in the development of the liturgy. If possible, opportunity ought to be provided to "run through" the action in place to get a feel for the acoustics and the visuals. There ought to be "tryouts" for readers and vocalists to learn the "feel" of the building and the liturgy. The organist or accompanist especially must be apprised of what is going on. (If the service should require a large number of hymns, such as the Good Friday service in this volume, it is advisable to paste the service together in a notebook from beginning to end that there be no awkward pauses between the readings, the versicles, and the hymns.)

Everyone and anyone involved in a new situation should have opportunity for a walk-through. A new crucifer or acolyte ought to be trained. Banner or pennon carriers should be rehearsed. If the choir processes, even they should be taught to walk like people approaching the throne room of the King. The recessional is no less important than the entrance.

Finally, the participating pastors must practice. It is one thing to repeat an order of worship every Sunday of the year. It is quite another to be faced with a new order without a notion of where it is going. When there is no one in the church nave, and those times come in huge blocks, the officiant ought to move through each phase of a new liturgy word by word, step by step, and turn by turn. When all is said and done, good order in the worship house is his most exquisite gift to his Lord.

The stonecraftsmen on the pinnacles of a cathedral tower carve the backs of angel heads as carefully as they carve the figures on the altar. No person may ever see the angel figure again once the scaffolding is removed. "But God sees it," they will tell you. One who does liturgy, either the writing or the leading of it, may have an indiscriminate congregation which is easily satisfied. Liturgy and worship are love offerings to a loving God.

CHRISTMAS

The Countdown Idea
Interludes—An Advent Countdown
Introduction to Worship on Christmas
A Christmas Candle Service
A Christmas Worship Service
Primer Thoughts for Christmas

The Countdown Idea

Candles in the church's Advent wreath are usually just lit with no particular acknowledgment of their presence. When the congregation gathers on the first Sunday in Advent, someone has managed to get the wreath in place. The acolyte strains to reach and light the first candle to mark the beginning of the new cycle. There is, of course, a whole excitement that goes with Advent I, and the candle is part of it; but what would happen if the candle were lit with a little ceremony all its own?

Here is a series of little ceremonies. They carry the title "Interlude" because they are designed to be an interlude in the worship service. The interlude could be placed before the Advent Lessons and Gospel or it might replace the postsermon hymn.

The original seven stanzas of "O come, O come, Emmanuel," based on the "O" Antiphons, are here reproduced. (They are not all used in most hymnals.) This or another time the "O" Antiphons could readily replace the suggested Collects.

The names of the candles are arbitrary. "Love, joy, peace, and hope" seemed appropriate, since they are gifts of God to His people by way of Jesus Christ. They could lead into a sermon series either during Advent or over the Christmas Feast.

A similar candle-lighting idea is suggested for the Easter-Pentecost cycle. That series of interludes is based on the seven gifts of the Holy Spirit (Isaiah 11:2).

Interlude
Countdown to Christmas (IV)

Love

The Hymn *(during which the "Love" candle is lit)* Latin, c. ninth century
Plainsong, Mode I

> O come, O come, Emmanuel
> And ransom captive Israel,
> That mourns in lonely exile here
> Until the Son of God appear.
> Rejoice! Rejoice! Emmanuel
> Shall come to thee, O Israel!

A Note

The delightful and traditional custom of lighting candles in a symbolic "Countdown to Christmas" begins this first Sunday in Advent. Except for the third candle, which is called "Gaudete" (Joy), no specific concepts are assigned to each candle. That fact allows anyone to name them how they will. This year, this first candle has been lit to symbolize the "Love" of God.

Our Lord, in His gift of Jesus Christ at Christmas, gave us the ultimate example of what it means "to love." God loved the world so: He gave up His only Son to die for it. Christ set the highest example of loving. For the joy of what He was doing for mankind, He set His face to go to Jerusalem. His cross is His life in action, an extension of His foot washing. It is His living out the eleventh commandment, "Thou shalt love thy God and thy neighbor."

The capacity to love is a gift and fruit of the Holy Spirit, Sanctifier, to any person who is in Jesus Christ. Because Christ was in them and in their midst, it was said of the early church, "Behold how they love each other." To the extent that Christ is in any of us, and to the extent that we as a community allow Him to be among us, to that extent we exercise this gift in our turn. May the love of Christ constrain us to love.

A Little Scripture   John 15:12-17

A Prayer

Holy Spirit, by whom the redemption of Jesus Christ is brought to the sinner and by whom alone faith in Jesus Christ is given to him, increase in us who profess our Christian faith the capacity to love our gracious Lord, each other, our enemies, and the world, that the purposes of the Father and the love of the Son are not thwarted

by our self-love; through Jesus Christ our Lord, with You and the Father, one God, with dominion over us forever. Amen.

The Hymn   Latin, c. ninth century
Plainsong, Mode I

> O come, Thou Wisdom from on high,
> Who ord'rest all things mightily;
> To us the path of knowledge show,
> And teach us in her ways to go.
> Rejoice! Rejoice! Emmanuel
> Shall come to thee, O Israel!

Interlude
Countdown to Christmas (III)
Love, Peace

The Hymn *(during which the "Peace" candle is lit)* Latin, c. ninth century
Plainsong, Mode I

> O come, O come, Thou Lord of might,
> Who to Thy tribes on Sinai's height
> In ancient times didst give the law,
> In cloud, and majesty, and awe.
> Rejoice! Rejoice! Emmanuel
> Shall come to thee, O Israel!

A Note

Our Lord created Adam and Eve in His own image. Whatever else the "image" may have been, our Lord's characteristics must be part of it. As He was love, they were; as He was gracious, and benevolent, they were. Thus, there was peace in the Garden of Eden.

Sin brought the loss of the image and consequently also of peace. Christ's redemption makes the image possible again. People, faithful to Him, seek in Him and by the Spirit's power to work for peace. It is not surprising to find "peace" a "Christmas gift," for peace is still the dream, the hope of God for His people, made possible through Christ, the Prince of Peace.

A Little Scripture   Isaiah 40:1-5

The Collect

Holy Spirit, who has called us by the Gospel, who enlightens us with gifts, and who sanctifies and keeps us in the holy faith, give us constantly the peace of God in Jesus Christ, our Lord, and help us to be peacemakers that we may be known by heaven and the world as sons and daughters of God; through Jesus Christ our Lord, with You and the Father, one God, with dominion over us forever. Amen.

The Hymn   Latin, c. ninth century
                                                Plainsong, Mode I

> O come, Desire of nations, bind
> In one the hearts of all mankind;
> Bid Thou our sad divisions cease,
> And be Thyself our King of Peace.
> Rejoice! Rejoice! Emmanuel
> Shall come to thee, O Israel!

Interlude
Countdown to Christmas (II)

Love, Peace, Joy

A Hymn *(during which the "Joy" candle is lit)*   Latin, c. ninth century
                                                Plainsong, Mode I

> O come, Thou Rod of Jesse's stem,
> From every foe deliver them
> That trust Thy mighty power to save,
> And give them vict'ry o'er the grave.
> Rejoice! Rejoice! Emmanuel
> Shall come to thee, O Israel!

A Note

The Christian has an advantage over the non-Christian; the person of faith is far better off than the person of non-faith. The faith-filled Christian knows Christ came; he knows Christ died for him; he knows that because Christ lives, he, too, will live. He knows God knows his humanness, his frailty, how tenuous his faith. So in his humanness he may weep at the death of a beloved one, but he rejoices with the saints in glory that a sinner has come home. He may cry for pain, physical and emotional, but he rejoices that God knows his predicament, and that He has sifted it through His fingers before ever it came to his life. The cross was certainly not of itself a joy to anticipate, but Christ, knowing He was obedient to His Father and the end result of His crucifixion for us, endured the cross "for the joy that was set before Him." Joy in the midst of this valley where the shadows are is truly a gift born out of the Christmas event.

A Little Scripture   Romans 5:1-5

A Collect

Holy Spirit, in whose province is the application of the forgiveness won on the cross and with it the assurance of everlasting life, keep our eyes upon the wonder of Christ and the glorious mansion God has opened to us, that in the midst of the vicissitudes and trials which may be our lot in time, we may be filled with all joy in believing and so pass this way in triumph, standing in anticipation of the joy yet to be ours in glory; through Jesus Christ our Lord, with You and the Father, one God, with dominion over us forever. Amen.

Thy Hymn   Latin, c. ninth century
                                                Plainsong, Mode I

> O come, Thou Key of David, come,
> And open wide our heav'nly home;
> Make safe the way that leads on high,
> And close the path to misery.
> Rejoice! Rejoice! Emmanuel
> Shall come to thee, O Israel!

Interlude
Countdown to Christmas (I)

Love, Peace, Joy, Hope!

The Hymn *(during which the "Hope" candle is lit)* Latin, c. ninth century
                                                Plainsong, Mode I

> O come, Thou Day-spring from on high,
> And cheer us by Thy drawing nigh;
> Disperse the gloomy clouds of night,
> And death's dark shadow put to flight.
> Rejoice! Rejoice! Emmanuel
> Shall come to thee, O Israel!

A Note

At the far end of the road—of life—of the world, Christ has promised many exciting things. The angels to carry us to glory, the approbation of the end-time Judge, the splendor of the throne room, the glory of the mansions, are some of them. God has made His monumental promises of mighty blessings in store for us. There they stand, these promises, and the pictures they evoke. God has planted hope for them into the hearts of His people. They are apprehended by faith. Faith reaches and grasps not only the Christ, but the hope of standing in the presence of God with Him.

Hope sustains God's people. In hope they have overcome persecution and martyrdom. In hope they have triumphed over long valley years. In hope they have laid loved ones into the bosom of the earth to wait for that great day of resurrection. Hope is one of our Lord's superb gifts to us, for His implanted hope must by the sheer reality of God be a realized hope.

Faith and hope are in a common bond. "Faith," writes the author to Hebrews, "Faith is the assurance of things hoped for, the conviction of things not seen" (Hebrews 11:1). Christmas and the birth of our Lord open the whole great gamut of faith and hope, promise and resolution laid before us by our loving God. It is fitting that one candle be labeled and symbolize hope.

A Little Scripture   Colossians 1:28—2:3

The Collect

Holy Spirit, who by the Word fires the imagination of God's people in anticipation of Christ's coming again to claim His own, lest, left to ourselves, we forfeit the glory and inherit hell, hold us firm in the holy faith and steady in our Christian hope against the day that Christ bursts forth in magnificent splendor to claim us for eternity; through Jesus Christ our Lord, with You and the Father, one God, with dominion over us forever. Amen.

The Hymn   Latin, c. ninth century
                                                    Plainsong, Mode I

O come, O come, Emmanuel,
And ransom captive Israel,
That mourns in lonely exile here
Until the Son of God appear.
Rejoice! Rejoice! Emmanuel
Shall come to thee, O Israel!

Introduction to Worship on Christmas

Christmas runs the gamut of possibilities for good worship. It is by its nature very folksy—a weary mother, a crowded inn, a Baby's first cry, and camels and a star—all stuff of the neighborhood. It is an awesome season, for the very Son of God has been made flesh to dwell among us, that we might behold in Him the glory of God. It is a joyous season, "For to us a Child is born, to us a Son is given."

Many congregations have more than one service over the Christmas Feast. The Feast's moods make possible different kinds of services. In addition, the sources of the past indicate a number of themes worth recapturing and building upon. The church of the Middle Ages saw Christmas happening in the dark, long nighttime of the year. "Light" as theme seemed to them a natural one. (Incidentally, the Christmas theme gives way to Easter and "Life," for Easter comes in the midst of budding trees and the first spring flowers.) Christmas is the birthday of King Jesus, which suggests another and ancient theme.

A sequence of Christmas services can be built around such a good theme. If, for instance, the chosen theme is "The King," activities centering around kings can determine the course of the Christmas celebration. At the king's birthday the peasants were treated to a celebration in the palace courtyard; the empire stood still until the announcement, "A king is born!" came from the balcony of the palace; the king granted audience and spoke his will to his subjects.

Or, if the theme is "Light," it is possible to divide the services (or a service) into "Light for a Quiet Night," "Light for a Dark Night," "Light After the Darkness." Each division gathers portions of the Light and expands them. The quiet night is the night our Lord was born. The dark night is the dark night of the soul for which our Lord left glory. Light after the darkness is the excitement that Christ lives and rules over us.

Exemplary services for divisions such as these are suggested in the following pages of Christmas celebrations. Some primer thoughts are included as aids to the serendipitous experience of discovering a new way to do the wonderful old "thing."

A Christmas Candle Service

"Light for a Dark Night"

Notes on the worship format for this Christmas Eve to help you in understanding your worship:

Just a few days ago the winter solstice passed, marking the longest night of the year. Whether by design or by accident, the celebration of the birth of Christ was placed in the long-dark-nights period. The symbolism, if it was not planned, was fortuitous; if it was planned, it was ingenious. It is in the dark night that the bright light of the celebration occurs, just as it is in the dark night of the soul that Christ's coming is as light. He is, in fact, the Light of the world, by His own choice of metaphor.

The service this holy night "capitalizes" on the darkness and Light symbolism and reality. The "darkness" keeps recurring, but as often as it returns, the Light strikes through it. The beginning of the service is in silence and darkness. The paschal candle (first lit on Holy Saturday to symbolize the risen Christ, and subsequently at Baptisms and funerals) enters the darkness first. The paschal candle is followed by people bearing lights, for all Christ's people are "candles." Finally the candles on the walls are lit, to suggest the dawn of a new day, the Dayspring from on high, driving the darkness back and away. Now the silence is broken with a paean of praise for the Light which has come to us in Christ.

Various themes, gathered under the main theme, now assert themselves. The Light is for a moment a candle in the mansion window, leading us through the darkness of time to glory. Now it is sun-Light breaking through the leaves of a fruit tree in Eden as Adam and Christ are contrasted. Again, it is the glow of an ancient city as Luke recounts the old, old story.

The service has two endings . . . the first in the reverie and quiet of "Silent night! Holy night!" Here visiting worshipers may leave. After the first conclusion, the Eucharist is celebrated. Touched by Christ in the Sacrament, the "candles of the Lord" pass the peace, then break into "Joy to the world, the Lord is come!" The Passing of the Peace is the Benediction.

"Light for a Dark Night"

The Order of Worship

The Prelude

The Theme: Symbolized

The Processional

From Darkness to Light

From Silence to Praise

A Carol   Nikolaus Herman
Lobt Gott, ihr Christen

Praise God the Lord, ye sons of men

The Theme: Candle in the Mansion Window

The Responsive Reading

Pastor: O Jesus
　　　Thou didst leave the councils
　　　　of the Trinity,

Thou didst consent to human form
　　in the virgin's womb,
Thou didst choose a stable for Thy birth,
Thou didst take the way to the cross,
Thou didst die beneath the crushing load
　　of our judgment.

People: Ah, Jesus, how didst Thou love us!
Pastor: O Christ,
　　　We are not worthy of Thy love.
　　　Our minds are filled with darkness,
　　　Our words oft betray our lovelessness,
　　　Our deeds are evil;
　　　We squander our time,
　　　We prostrate our talents,
　　　We divide our treasures far too carefully,
　　　Because we are more Adam's children than Thine,
　　　Because we belong more to ourselves than to Thee.
People: Canst Thou love us still, dear Lord?
Pastor: Thou dost come to us on the wings of memory
　　　as we celebrate Thy birth into time.
　　　Thy sighing, groaning, bleeding, dying,
　　　　burns in our minds and hearts,
　　　Thy Word with tender forgiveness
　　　　in its deepest core covers us, and
　　　Thy plenteous grace and tender mercy
　　　　well over us.
　　　We are cleansed of our unrighteousness;
　　　　we are freed of our sins.
People: Aye, Jesus, Thou dost love us still.
Pastor: Thou dost daily purge our hearts of sin,
　　　Thou dost fill us full with faith,
　　　Thou dost continually intercede
　　　　at the judgment seat for us.
　　　Thou dost warm us with Thy love,
　　　Thou dost permeate us with hope,
　　　Thou dost cover us in Thy peace.
People: Thy peace Thou hast left with us;
　　　Thy peace hast Thou gives us.
　　　Amen and Amen.

The Lesson   Galatians 4:4-6

The Anthem

The Theme: Sunlight Through a Fruit Tree

An Affirmation of the Faith   From Romans 5:12-22
                                                   Adapted from Phillips

Pastor: As a result of Adam's sin, death became the common lot of men.

People: By the generosity of God, by the free giving of the grace of Jesus Christ, the love of God overflowed for our benefit.

Pastor: Adam's sin brought judgment and condemnation upon us all.

People: Through Jesus Christ our sin is met with the free gift of grace and justification before God.

Pastor: Adam's sin condemned us all to a lifetime of slavery and to death.

People: Through Jesus Christ, we, by our acceptance of His grace and righteousness, live our lives like royalty.

Pastor: As one act of sin exposed all of us to God's judgment and death,

People: so one act of perfect righteousness acquits us all in the sight of God.

Pastor: One man's disobedience led to hell;

People: but one Man's obedience has the power to present us righteous before God.

Pastor: Sin is wide and deep;

People: God's grace is wider and deeper still!

Pastor: Sin used to be the master of men and in the end handed them over to death;

People: now grace is the ruling factor, righteousness is its purpose, and bringing us to eternal life with God through Jesus Christ our Lord is its end.

Pastor: While we were yet sinners,

People: Christ died for us.

Pastor: While we were yet enemies,

People: Christ reconciled us to God.

Pastor: While we are yet sinners,

People: we are saints through the grace of our Lord Jesus Christ.

The Hymn   Charles Wesley
                                                   Mendelssohn

Christ by highest heav'n adored
(Stanza 2 of Hark! the herald angels sing)

The Theme: Glow from an Ancient City

The Gospel   Luke 2:1-7

The Solo

The Theme: Out of the Darkness, Light

The Meditation

The Offering

An Anthem

The Prayers

The Theme: Light on the Edge of the Darkness

A Responsive Reading   Selected Scripture
                                                   Adapted from *The Jerusalem Bible*

Pastor: God is Light;

People: there is no darkness in Him at all.

Pastor: If we say that we are in union with God while we are living in darkness, we are lying because we are not living the truth.

People: But if we live our lives in the Light, as He is in the Light, we are in union with one another, and the blood of Jesus, His Son, purifies us from all sin.

Pastor: Though the night still covers the earth and darkness the peoples of it,

People: arise, shine out, for your Light has come, the glory of the Lord is rising upon you.

Pastor: Above you the Lord God now rises and over you His glory appears.

People: The nations come to your Light and kings to your dawning brightness.

Pastor: No more will the sun give you daylight, nor moonlight shine on you,

People: but the Lord will be your everlasting Light, your God will be your Splendor.

Pastor: The sun will set no more, nor the moon wane,

People: but the Lord will be your everlasting Light and our days of mourning will be ended.

Pastor: Man's spirit is the lamp of the Lord.

People: Let us shine in the dark world like bright stars, to offer the world the Word of life.

Pastor: You are the light of the world.

People: May our light shine so that men give praise to our Father in heaven.

Pastor: All that comes to be has life in Christ, and that life is the Light of men,

People: a Light that shines in the dark, a Light that darkness cannot overpower.

Pastor: The new Jerusalem does not need the sun or the moon for light.

People: It is lit by the radiant glory of God and the Lamb is a lighted torch for it.

Pastor: It will never be night again and the saints will need no lamp or sunlight;

People: the Lord God will be shining upon them.

Pastor: The Lamb that was sacrificed is worthy to be given power, riches and wisdom, strength and honor, glory and blessing.

People: To the One who is sitting on the throne and to the Lamb, be all praise and honor, glory and power, for ever and ever.

Pastor: Amen and Amen.

People: Amen and Amen.

A Carol   Joseph Mohr
                                                Stille Nacht

                    Silent night! Holy night!

A Collect for Peace

The Benediction

The Recessional

                            Interlude

            The Theme: Light for the Night of the Soul

The Hymn   Jaroslav Vajda
                                                    Now

            Now the silence Now the peace

The Consecration

The Confession of our Sinfulness   (The Night)

Pastor and People: O almighty God, merciful Father, I, a poor, miserable sinner, confess unto Thee all my sins and iniquities with which I have ever offended Thee and justly deserved Thy temporal and eternal punishment. But I am heartily sorry for them and sincerely repent of them, and I pray Thee of Thy boundless mercy and for the sake of the holy, innocent, bitter sufferings and death of Thy beloved Son, Jesus Christ, to be gracious and merciful to me, a poor, sinful being.

(What do we mean by a Sacrament? By a Sacrament we mean a sacred act—instituted by God Himself; in which there are certain visible means connected with His Word; and by which God offers, gives, and seals unto us the forgiveness of sins which Christ has earned for us.)

The Distribution   (The Light)

(During the Distribution, a quiet rehearsal of the old favorites among the carols.)

                The Theme: Symbolized

                The Light of Christmas

The Passing of the Peace

            (In the midst of the Passing of the Peace, the Carol)

                                                Isaac Watts
                                                    Antioch

            Joy to the world, the Lord is come!

A Christmas Worship Service

                "Light After the Darkness"

Notes on the origin of the worship format for this Christmas morning, and for the doing of it:

Two major concepts dominated the festival season of the church year in the historical church, both of which are still valid. During the Christmas and Epiphany cycles the overriding theme is LIGHT. The theme for Lent, Easter, and Pentecost is LIFE.

Right there is an excellent concept on which to base our worship this year—LIGHT! Darkness and Light! The whole idea is a dominating one in Scripture (He has "called you out of darkness into His marvelous light. Once you were no people but now you are God's people; once you had not received mercy but now you have received mercy" [1 Peter 2:9-10]).

Thus the service this morning was born and grew following the darkness-light motif. Once the announcement of the day is made and the call to worship (this morning, the processional hymn) has been sounded, the motif is explored in various ways. The negative is contrasted with the positive, confession with absolution, the historical Christmas Psalm, De Profundis, with a powerful Christmas carol, the nighttime of the Christmas story with the bright-time of paradise. An interlude of LIGHT intrudes to break the rhythm in the center portion. Then, once more the motif asserts itself, this time God's pronouncement against sinful humanity in Eden as man's darkest night is transcended by the thrilling words of a "judgment hymn" set to the king of the choral tunes. Here is the final statement of our triumph in Jesus, our Savior. Then, at the end, the dismissal.

There is a certain drama in worship. Please allow yourself to be caught up in the drama as well as the worship! The organist will "cue you in" as to when to begin the next statement set to music. The drama happens when the assertion of light triumphs over darkness, when the affirmation of Christ supersedes the affirmation of our unworthiness. Thus the drama unfolds without rehearsal; and, with the blessing of the Holy Spirit, good worship will happen, whereby our King, the Christ, is glorified; our Lord, the Father, is praised; and we are blessed because of it.

Christmas Day
"Light After the Darkness"
The Order of Worship

The Prelude

The Proclamation   (From the Magnificat Antiphons)

Pastor: This day Christ was born, this day the Savior has appeared.
    This day the angels are singing on earth, and the archangels are rejoicing through all the reaches of heaven.
    This day the just exult and sing: Glory to God in the highest! Alleluia!

The Processional and Call to Worship   Author unknown
Adeste fideles

Oh, come, all ye faithful, triumphantly sing

The Announcement of the Motif for Worship   (1 Peter 2:9-10)

Pastor: But you are a chosen race, a royal priesthood, a holy nation. God's own people, that you may declare the wonderful deeds of Him who called you out of darkness into His marvelous light. Once you were no people but now you are God's people; once you had not received mercy but now you have received mercy.
People: God has called us out of darkness into His marvelous light. Hallelujah!

The Confession and Absolution—the first experience of the night-day motif
Pastor: Let us kneel and make confession of our sins before God.

Darkness

Pastor and People: Eternal God, our Judge and Redeemer; we confess that we have tried to hide from You, for we have done wrong. We have lived for ourselves. We have refused to shoulder the troubles of others, and have turned from our neighbors. We have ignored the pain of others, and passed by the hungry, the poor, and the cold. O God, in Your great mercy, forgive our sin and free us from our selfishness, that we may choose Your will and obey Your commandments; through Jesus Christ our Lord. Amen.

Light

Pastor: God shows His love for us, in that while we were yet sinners, Christ was born in Bethlehem, Christ lived under the Law for us, Christ went under judgment for us, Christ died for us. The mercy of God and of His Christ is from everlasting to everlasting. I declare unto you, in the name of Jesus Christ, that as we have confessed our sins, and affirmed the holy name of Christ as Savior, we are forgiven.
Pastor and People: Amen.

The Psalmody—the second experience of the motif

Darkness

Psalm 130 *(a psalm often read at requiem, yet appointed for Christmas)*

Light

The Anthem Carol

The Gospel—the third experience of the motif

Night

Luke 2

Day

The Carol   Nikolaus Herman
Lobt Gott, ihr Christen

Praise God the Lord, ye sons of men

The Epistle—the fourth experience of the motif

Sin

Romans 7:14-24

Grace

Our Affirmation on Sonship (together)   (Galatians 4:4-7)

But when the time had fully come, God sent forth His Son, born of woman, born under the law, to redeem those who were under the Law, so that we might receive adoption as sons. And because you are sons, God has sent the Spirit of His Son into our hearts, crying, "Abba! Father!" So through God you are no longer a slave but a son, and if a son then an heir.

Interlude

The Office Hymn   Philipp Nicolai
Wie Schoen leuchtet

How lovely shines the Morning Star!
(Selected stanzas)

The Message

The Offering

The Prayers

The Anthem

Interlude ends

The Gloom and the Glory—a final statement and affirmation of the motif

The Gloom

Genesis 3:14-20

The Splendor

The Hymn   Philipp Nicolai
Wachet auf

Wake, awake, for night is flying

(Stanza 3)

The Epilog

The Collect for Peace
The Benediction
The Recessional Hymn   The Quempas Celebration
(A 14-century carol)

Primer Thoughts for Christmas

Here are a few suggestions for multiple services holding to a single theme:

1. The Family

   A. The Family at Christmas
      (A "folksy" celebration with the children, junior choirs, guitars, as the families of the congregation gather for worship. A little sermon with a visual aid with the children in mind.)

   B. The Holy Family at Christmas *("God has placed the Solitary in the family")*
      (In the hush of the holy night, in which the O Antiphons are prayed between stanzas of "O come, O come, Emmanuel," the holy Child and His parents of Bethlehem are center for a moment, and in which the Savior Christ comes in the blessed Sacrament.)

   C. The Whole Family at Christmas
      (In which our familyhood in Jesus Christ is established [Gal. 4:4-7], the birth of Christ is commemorated, and the highest and finest Member of the family of God and the family of the church is celebrated.)

2. The Gift

   A. God the Father, Giver of the Perfect Gift
      (A service in praise of the love that moved the Father to give the Gift. The service might be kept "light" by beginning the sermon with the announcement of Christ's birth. Then briefly the problem Christmas has had with the intruding "folksy" quality. Troubadours interrupt the sermon to sing of and recite the happy joy of Christmas. The sermon resumes to speak of the meaning of it all.)

   B. God the Son, Gift of the Perfect Giver
      (In which the Christmas story is told and retold—by Isaiah, by Luke, by Paul, by John, each one emphasizing the splendor of the Gift, all woven through with carols and anthems.)

   C. God the Holy Spirit, Who Makes Delivery of the Gift
      (In which adoration, praise, and thanksgiving for the Gift are offered, in obedience to, and in the power of, the Holy Spirit.)

3. Christ and the Kingdoms

   A. Christ and the Kingdom of Power
      (A general theme offering opportunity for the "folksy" approach. There are many happy things the royal citizenry can do—a carol sing, a miracle play,

songs of the little children. Many people won't observe the birthday of our King, but those of us who know—we will; we must.)

B. Christ and the Kingdom of Grace
(Jesus is the church community's King. All the citizenry have received His grace and live by faith in Him. People, not geography, define the Kingdom's boundaries. The mark of the Kingdom is freedom under Christ. The throne room doors are open wide. The citizenry can pay Him homage, accept His offer for an audience, offer Him gifts, petition Him, and celebrate His Lordship— all in the name of Christmas!)

C. Christ and the Kingdom of Glory
(The King came in a "size everyone can handle" in Bethlehem, but who can grasp the concept "King of kings and Lord of lords"? Who will believe that the King of kings "lay thus in lowly manger"? Yet He was incarnate. Even now He reigns and rules. This is a day to worship the King of kings in majesty, to hear His pronouncements, to learn again His love.)

EPIPHANY

Notes on Epiphany
An Event for Epiphany
(Or for Christ the King Sunday)
Primer Thoughts for Epiphany

Notes on Epiphany

Epiphany, the twelfth day after Christmas, celebrates the visit of the Wise Men who came in search of the newborn King. Emphasis for a service may land at various places in the Epiphany service. Since an "epiphany" was the visit of a king or dignitary to his people, the visit of the King of kings to our small planet is an event to commemorate and celebrate. Here is a responsive reading suggested for an Epiphany service. Fit it into vespers. Add banners or pennons. Splice in several of the Epiphany hymns or choir anthems. Let the Kings of kings emerge through the power of the Word. Let all the people praise Him at His appearing.

An Event for Epiphany
(Or for Christ the King Sunday)

(The readings are from *The New Testament in Modern English*, translated by J. B. Phillips. The people's responses are selected paeans of praise from Revelation, RSV.)

Christ the King

First and Upholding Principle

Leader: He is both the first principle and the upholding principle of the whole scheme of creation. And now He is the Head of the body which is the church. Life from nothing began through Him, and life from the dead began through Him, and He is, therefore, justly called the Lord of all. (Colossians 1:17-18)

People: Amen! Blessing and glory and wisdom and thanksgiving and honor and power and might be to our God forever and ever! Amen! (Revelation 7:12)

Christ the King

Who Gave Himself for Us

Leader: Here is the High Priest we need. A Man who is holy, faultless, unstained, beyond the very reach of sin and lifted above the very heavens. There is no need for Him, like the high priests we know, to offer up daily sacrifices, first for His own sins and then for the people's. He made one sacrifice, once for all, when He offered up Himself. The Law makes for its high priests men of human weakness. But the word of the oath, which came after the Law, makes for High Priest the Son, who is perfect forever! (Hebrews 7:26-28)

People: Salvation belongs to our God who sits upon the throne, and to the Lamb! (Revelation 7:10)

Christ the King

of Tremendous Majesty

Leader: This Son, radiance of the glory of God, flawless expression of the nature of God, Himself the upholding principle of all that is, effected in person the reconciliation between God and man and then took His seat at the right hand of the majesty on high—thus proving Himself, by the more glorious name that He has won, far greater than all the angels of God. (Hebrews 1:3-4)

People: Worthy is the Lamb who was slain, to receive power and wealth and wisdom and might and honor and glory and blessing! (Revelation 5:12)

Christ the King

of Glorious Triumph

Leader: The glorious fact is that Christ *did* rise from the dead: He has become the very first to rise of all who sleep the sleep of death. As death entered the world through a man, so has rising from the dead come to us through a Man! As members of a sinful race all men die; as members of the Christ of God all men shall be raised to life, each in his proper order, with Christ the very first and after Him all who belong to Him when He comes.

Then, and not till then, comes the end when Christ, having abolished all other rule, authority and power, hands over the Kingdom to God the Father. Christ's reign will and must continue until every enemy has been conquered. The last enemy of all to be destroyed is death itself. (1 Corinthians 15:20-26)

People: To Him who sits upon the throne and to the Lamb be blessing and honor and glory and might forever and ever! (Revelation 5:13)

Christ the King

Our Brother

Leader: For now that you have faith in Christ Jesus you are all sons of God. All of you who were baptized "into" Christ have put on the family likeness of Christ. Gone is the distinction between Jew and Greek, slave and free man, male and female—you are all one in Christ Jesus! And if you belong to Christ, you are true descendants of Abraham, you are true heirs of his promise. (Galatians 3:26-29)

People: Great and wonderful are Thy deeds, O Lord God the Almighty! Just and true are Thy ways, O King of the ages! Who shall not fear and glorify Thy name, O Lord? For Thou alone art holy. All nations shall come and worship Thee, for Thy judgments have been revealed. (Revelation 15:3-4)

Christ the King

Our Champion

Leader: Even though we were dead in our sins, God, who is rich in mercy, because of the great love He had for us, gave us life together with Christ—it is, remember, by grace and not by achievement that you are saved—and has lifted us right out of the old life to take our place with Him in Christ Jesus in the Heavens. Thus He shows for all time the tremendous generosity of the grace and kindness He has expressed toward us in Christ Jesus. It was nothing you could or did achieve—it was God's gift of grace which saved you. (Ephesians 2:4-8)

People: Hallelujah! For the Lord our God the Almighty reigns. Let us rejoice and exult and give Him the glory, for the marriage of the Lamb has come, and His bride has made herself ready. (Revelation 19:6-7)

Christ the King

Our Leader in Battle

Leader: In conclusion, be strong—not in yourselves but in the Lord, in the power of His boundless resource. Put on God's complete armor so that you can successfully resist all the devil's methods of attack. For our fight is not against any physical enemy: it is against organizations and powers that are spiritual. We are up against the unseen power that controls this dark world, and spiritual agents from the very headquarters of evil. Therefore you must wear the whole armor of God that you may be able to resist evil in its day of power, and that even when you have fought to a standstill you may still stand your ground. Take your stand then with truth as your belt, righteousness your breastplate, the gospel of peace firmly on your feet, salvation as your helmet and in your hand the sword of the Spirit, the Word of God. Above all be sure you take faith as your shield, for it can quench every burning missile the enemy hurls at you. Pray at all times with every kind of spiritual prayer, keeping alert and persistent as you pray for all Christ's men and women. (Ephesians 6:10-18)

People: Behold, He is coming with the clouds, and every eye will see Him, every one who pierced Him; and all tribes of the earth will wail on account of him. Even so. Amen. (Revelation 1:7)

Christ the King

Victor

Leader: Then one of the seven angels who hold the seven bowls which were filled with the seven last plagues came to me and said, "Come, and I will show you the bride, the wife of the Lamb."

Then he carried me away in spirit to the top of a vast mountain, and pointed out to me the city, the holy Jerusalem, descending from God out of heaven, radiant with the glory of God. Her brilliance sparkled like a very precious jewel with the clear light of crystal. Around her she had a vast and lofty wall in which were twelve gateways with twelve angels at the gates. . . . The wall of the city had twelve foundation stones and on these were engraved the names of the twelve apostles of the Lamb.

I could see no Temple in the city, for the Lord, the almighty God, and the Lamb are Themselves its Temple. The city has no need for the light of the sun or moon, for the splendor of God fills it with light, and its radiance is the Lamb. The nations will walk by its light, and the kings of the earth will bring their glory into it. The city's gates shall stand open day after day—and there will be no night there. Into the city

they will bring the splendors and honors of the nations. (Revelation 21:9-14; 22-26)

People: Worthy is the Lamb who was slain, to receive power and wealth and wisdom and might and honor and glory and blessing! (Revelation 5:12)

To Him who sits upon the throne and to the Lamb be blessing and honor and glory and might forever and ever! (Revelation 5:13)

Great and wonderful are Thy deeds,
   O Lord God the Almighty!
Just and true are Thy ways,
   O King of the ages!
Who shall not fear and glorify Thy name,
   O Lord? For Thou alone art holy.
   (Revelation 15:3b-4)
Praise our God, all you His servants,
   you who fear Him, small and great.
   (Revelation 19:5b)
Hallelujah!
   For the Lord our God the Almighty reigns.
   (Revelation 19:6b)

Primer Thoughts for Epiphany

Or here is an order in outline of a simple service for Epiphany. It lends itself to the tree-undercoating, tree-burning Twelfth Night.

Theme: The Star

1. Sighting the Star

—with a hymn   Philipp Nicolai
                                                    Wie schoen leuchtet

How lovely shines the Morning Star!

—with Scripture: Revelation 22:1-5, 16

—with prayer

2. Remembering the Star

—with Scripture: Matthew 2:1-2

—and song   John H. Hopkins, Jr.
                                                    Kings of Orient

We three kings of Orient are
(Stanza 1 and chorus)

Matthew 2:3-10

Born a King on Bethlehem's plain
(Stanzas 2—4)

Matthew 2:12

Glorious now behold Him arise
(Stanza 5)

3. The Star Beckons

—with Scripture: Matthew 4:18-22

—with a hymn   Johann Scheffler
                                         Mach's mit mir, Gott

Come, follow Me, the Savior spake

4. We Follow the Star

—with a prayer

—with a hymn   Charles S. Robinson
                                              Winterton

Savior, I follow on

5. The Star Leads

—with Scripture: Isaiah 60:1-15

—with a hymn   Hermann Fick
                                               O du Liebe

Rise, Thou Light of Gentile nations

6. The Star Is Still At Last

—with Scripture: Revelation 21:1-5; 22-25

—with a hymn   Philipp Nicolai
                                        Wie schoen leuchtet

Oh, joy to know that Thou, my Friend
("How lovely shines the Morning Star," stanza 7)

7. Conclusion

—The Collect for Peace
—The Benediction
—Holding the Star   Mary F. Maude
                                                Vienna

Thine forever, God of Love!

PALM SUNDAY

Notes on Palm Sunday
A Palm Sunday Service
Primer Thoughts for Palm Sunday

Notes on Palm Sunday

Palm Sunday is an exciting day in the cycle of great days in the church. Jesus is in command of the day from beginning to end. He commandeers a donkey without let or hindrance from some unknown man. He receives the accolades of the people. He is feted by the children. He is Master in His Father's house as He drives the moneychangers from their booths.

But the day is His master, as well. There is a goodly element of those who stood on the sidelines who caviled about the adoration. St. Luke questions the adoration, for it appears to him that the triumph and accolades depended on "the mighty works which they had seen." The moneychangers ran to the high priest, who, seeing the threat in this Jesus of Nazareth to the whole religious structure, not to mention his own pocketbook, must certainly have renewed his determination that this "one Man should die for the people"!

Another fact overpowers the day. Perhaps the events of Palm Sunday were predetermined. Jesus, who knew the precise time that "His hour had come" to change water into wine, knew also that the time had now come for His demise at Jerusalem. A Palm Sunday service may not mention it, but that fact must permeate any worship on that day. It may, on the other hand, dominate it!

Through the centuries, the church has been conscious of the faithful Christians, especially those who were martyred and, like the white-robed multitudes carrying palm branches in John's vision, have entered glory through much tribulation. The palm branch custom grew as much out of the palm-carrying martyrs as from the branch-strewing Jerusalemites.

Out of thoughts like these the stuff of worship can be fabricated. The sermon can be caught in the vortex of the carefully constructed liturgy. The Eucharist, should it be celebrated, can be affirmation or healing, or benediction, depending on the liturgy's emphasis. Palm Sunday is an exciting day!

A Palm Sunday Service
Notes Anticipating This Service

Palm Sunday, the gateway to Holy Week, is first of all the memorial to our Lord's entrance into Jerusalem. This festive parade was His wedding march as He proceeded to seal with blood His Bridegroom's love for the human family.

It is, furthermore, a feast in honor of Christ the King. This is the first time during His earthly life that He allowed royal homage to be paid Him. On the basis of His kingship He was convicted and sentenced to die. He was a martyr to His royal title.

But Palm Sunday brings us face to face with suffering, for it introduces us to Christ's sacred Passion. We are to share our Master's burden. The liturgy therefore is quite "dramatic." Christ is in our midst, and by our actions we proclaim ourselves His disciples. We accompany Him along the road from Mount Olivet to the city gate, into the Holy City to stand with Him before His executioners, and finally outside the city walls to Golgotha to watch Him expire.

This service has been carefully constructed to achieve these historic and traditional Palm Sunday themes. At the beginning there are songs of praise. There is the Palm Sunday message for this day in the proclaimed Word. Finally, there is the consecration of the palms and the blessing of those who carry them.

The service ends with "The Procession," used for the first time at our church, in which the worshipers, carrying palms, follow the cross out of the church into the world. The symbolism is this: as soldiers and martyrs of Christ, we accompany the Lord and King of martyrs into the strife (herein lies the real significance of the palms). This is a procession to honor the Conqueror over death and hell as He proceeds to the battlefield. Christians are marching with Christ, a train of heroes and conquerors!

The palms traditionally are taken home and placed where they can be a quiet reminder of the assurance of God's grace and of our commitment to Him.

The Sunday of the Passion

Palm Sunday

The Order of Worship

The Prelude

The Processional

Georg Weissel
Macht hoch die Tuer

Lift up your heads, ye mighty gates!

The Call to Worship on the Sunday of the Passion   (Selected KJV)

Pastor: Open to me the gates of righteousness; I will go into them, and I will praise the Lord.

People: This is the day which the Lord hath made. We will rejoice and be glad in it.

Pastor: Blessed is He that cometh in the name of the Lord; we have blessed You out of the house of the Lord.

People: O give thanks unto the Lord: for He is good: for His mercy endureth forever.

Pastor: Rejoice greatly, O daughter of Zion; shout, O daughter of Jerusalem; behold, thy King cometh unto thee;

People: He is just and having salvation; lowly and riding on a donkey. Now is the Son of Man glorified and God is glorified in Him.

Pastor: God hath highly exalted Him, and given Him a name which is above every name; that at the name of Jesus every knee should bow, of things in heaven and things in earth, and things under the earth; and that every tongue should confess:

People: Jesus Christ is Lord, to the glory of God the Father.

Pastor: Rejoice greatly, O daughter of Zion, behold, thy King cometh unto thee.

People: Blessed is He that cometh in the name of the Lord.

The Confession of Sins

Pastor: Beloved in Christ Jesus: I call upon you to confess your sins before Him and to receive from Him the forgiveness which He merited for you on the cross.

Pastor: For living less than the reconciled life,

People: Forgive us, O Lord.

Pastor: For neglecting the privileges of prayer,

People: Forgive us, O Lord.

Pastor: For being too busy to hear You speak,

People: Forgive us, O Lord.

Pastor: For the limitation on our trust,

People: Forgive us, O Lord.

Pastor: For our spiritual inertia,

People: Forgive us, O Lord.

Pastor: For doubting the mystery,
People: Forgive us, O Lord.
Pastor: For saying yes and failing to act,
People: Forgive us, O Lord.
Pastor: For saying no and not meaning it,
People: Forgive us, O Lord.
Pastor: For our fear of involvement,
People: Forgive us, O Lord.
Pastor: For the uncommitted part of us,
People: Forgive us, O Lord.
Pastor: For our spotty loving,
People: Forgive us, O Lord.
Pastor: For our gloomy thoughts,
People: Forgive us, O Lord.
Pastor: For neglecting the needy,
People: Forgive us, O Lord.
Pastor: For demeaning our gifts,
People: Forgive us, O Lord.
Pastor: For our inopportune silences,
People: Forgive us, O Lord.
Pastor: For our level of gratitude,
People: Forgive us, O Lord.
Pastor: And for our poverty of praise,
People: Forgive us, O Lord.

The Absolution

Pastor: God shows His love for us, in that while we were yet
sinners, Christ died for us.
The mercy of the Father is from everlasting to
everlasting.
I declare to you, in the name of Jesus Christ, we are
forgiven.
People: Amen.

The Collect

Hosanna to You, redeeming Lord, whose procession of triumph
climaxed on the hill of Calvary; for You, who are truly the Son of God,
held steady to Your course until in dying You accomplished Your holy
purpose, the world's redemption. Hosanna to the Son of the living
God; who with the Father and the Spirit, alone are worthy of our
praise and adoration. Amen.

The Hymn	James Montgomery
	Innocents

Songs of praise the angels sang

The First Lesson	Zechariah 9:9-12
The Second Lesson	Philippians 2:5-11
The Anthem	
The Gospel	Mark 11:1-10
The Office Hymn	Hans A. Brorson
	Der lieben Sonne Licht und Pracht

I walk in danger all the way

The Sermon	
The Offering	
The Prayer	
The Hymn	Henry H. Milman
	Winchester New

Ride on, ride on, in majesty!

The Consecration of the Palm Branches

Pastor: Blessed is the King who comes in the name of the Lord.
People: Peace in heaven and glory in the highest.
Pastor: The Lord be with you.
People: And also with you.
Pastor: Let us give thanks to the Lord our God.
People: It is right to give Him thanks and praise.
Pastor: I set these palm branches apart as a memorial to the
triumphal entry of our Lord into Jerusalem. May they serve
the people of this community of Christ's people as a memorial
to His kingship.
I set these palm branches apart as a sign of the victory of
Christ over the wrath of God, over sin and the Law and over
death. May they be a remembrance among us of His holy
priesthood.
I set these palm branches apart as a symbol among us,
each to the other and before God, of our commitment to
Christ who redeemed us. May they who carry the palm
branches understand their symbolism, giving honor and
praise to the King of kings for the privilege granted us in our
election and our faith.

Let us confess our faith in the triune God.

The Apostles' Creed

The Prayer

Pastor: It is right to praise You, almighty God, for the acts of love by which You have redeemed us through Your Son, Jesus Christ, our Lord. We recall how He entered the holy city of Jerusalem in triumph, and was proclaimed as King by those who spread their garments and branches of palm along His way. Let these branches be for us signs of His victory, and grant that we who bear them in His name may ever hail Him as our King, and follow Him in the way that leads to eternal life; who lives and reigns in glory with You and the Holy Spirit, now and forever.

People: Amen.

Pastor: Blessed is He who comes in the name of the Lord.

People: Hosanna in the highest.

The Benediction

The Procession

(Members of the worshiping community will proceed from the rear rows down the two outside aisles. At the altar steps they will receive a palm. They are to fall into the "Procession" behind the crucifer or choir, and proceed out of the nave and the building. As the Procession of the committed Christians moves out of the gathering place to the world they sing:)

The Recessional Procession Hymn   St. Theodulph of Orleans
Valet will ich dir geben

All glory, laud, and honor

(Outside, a Second Benediction)
Please, let us wish each other well as we return to homes and work-places and play-places, that each of us may be faithful to Christ in every place.)

Primer Thoughts for Palm Sunday

The thoughts swirling around the triumphal entry into Jerusalem are like a busy traffic circle. There are themes and undercurrents and motifs that make for exciting worship on Palm Sunday. Here are two more suggestions.

1. The hymn, "All glory, laud, and honor," the only surviving hymn of Theodulph of Orleans (c. 760—821) suggests possibilities, especially from the historical usage and legend that surround it. In times past the day was filled with procession and pageantry, with children's choirs and anthems, with prayers for the city and the land. There is latitude in these post-Easter times to celebrate the Palm Sunday event with sheer and exciting praise.

2. But Palm Sunday is also full of tensions. A respectable service can be built out of the tensions. Jesus is riding amid praise and glad "Hosannas" to hell. The tensions can be demonstrated by what the congregation does juxtapositioned by what the choir does. The congregation might read a psalm of praise only to be drawn into the tension as the choir sings a Lenten hymn ("Go to dark Gethsemane," for instance) in counterpoint. The congregation might listen to the Gospel for the day, only to sing "O darkest woe" in black-white contrast. The cross draws Christ inexorably into its open maw. Palm Sunday is no relief on the journey.

MAUNDY THURSDAY

Notes on Maundy Thursday Worship
A Narrative Communion
for Maundy Thursday
Primer Thoughts for Maundy Thursday

Notes on Maundy Thursday Worship

Commemoration of the night in which our Lord was betrayed is very much in order. The upper room discourses and the "High Priestly" prayer are sublime. The institution of the Eucharist as a Sacrament to be done "in remembrance of" Him fairly begs the repetition of it on the traditional night of its origin. The high drama of the confrontation of the paschal lamb and Christ, our Passover, needs constant reviewing. The establishment of the "new covenant in My blood," to replace the old Sinaitic covenant born in thunder and fear, offers profound opportunity to rejoice in the Gospel. The family gathers around its Head Master at the holy table, eager to know again His gentle touch in the bread and wine, and to hold hands each with the other in the wonder of community. Here at the table is the Christian church as its deepest and most sacred moment.

Many attempts have been made to link the Seder and the Maundy Thursday celebration of the Sacrament. Through an "historian" the attempt presented here picks up the Passover lamb as a type of Christ, recounts the divine directives for the lamb, presents the city scene at that fatal Passover, finally singling out one lamb to be spitted, roasted, and served at the upper room commemoration. Interwoven with the historian's account is the running commentary on the salvation history recounted in the mass. The historian's narration concludes at the table in the upper room; the commentator's remarks continue; for Christ, our Passover sacrificed for us, is yet to be memorialized and His presence experienced.

This services takes liberty with the Confession and Absolution. Instead of appearing at the beginning of the service, it will appear at the Good Friday memorial and immediately preceding the "Easter" event. It is not disconcerting, for it brings into sharp focus the purpose of the cross and the splendor of the Resurrection.

A Narrative Communion for Maundy Thursday

Notes Before the Service

For a thousand years the Hebrews celebrated the Passover to commemorate the "saving event" in their history. The ritual called for bitter herbs and wine, but most it called for a lamb. The paschal lamb reminded them of how a lamb's blood, painted on the lintels of their fathers' doorways, had saved their fathers from the angel of death that fateful night in Egypt; the herbs recalled their bitter suffering in the wilderness and through the centuries following.

In the strange way our Lord has of reaching in both directions at one time, He allowed the covenant people to draw their identity from the Passover/Red Sea experience, but He used the event as a "sign" of the salvation to come. The lamb of the Passover was sign for the true Paschal Lamb, Jesus Christ. It is questionable whether the Hebrew saw the connection, but in the total perspective of God's plan of salvation the "sign" is unmistakable.

The worship experience tonight is hopefully enhanced by superimposing the Old Testament concepts of the lamb on the New Testament form our worship in Holy Communion has taken. The Old commemorates the sign; the New celebrates the Reality. The one is prophetic; the other is fulfillment. Two narrators will trace the themes. Their comments will separate and converge, touching at last in the awesome moment of confrontation in the Passover in the upper room, that night in which our Lord was betrayed. After that the "sign" is finished; the "Reality" is placed on the altar of Calvary's hill, where He gives His life for the world. No longer now do we paint blood on the lintels of the doorways to our homes; now the blood of the Paschal Lamb is, by faith, upon the doorway of our heart.

May the narration during the service add a little more to your understanding of the Sacrament, and deepen your worship during this hour.

> "Christ our Passover is sacrificed for us.
> Alleluia!"

Maundy Thursday

The Order of Worship

The Organ Prelude

The Introduction of the Themes

Theme A: The Historian
The Sign, the Paschal Lamb   (Exodus 12:1-4)

Theme B: The Interpreter
           The Reality, The Christ   (Galatians 4:4-7)

The Entrance (The Processional)   Psalms 118, 114

(These two entrance Psalms are from the Hillel Psalms [113—118] sung at the Passover, and undoubtedly used by our Lord the night in which He was betrayed.)

Psalm 118 (TJB)

A Processional Hymn for the Feast of Tabernacles

Pastor: Give thanks to Yahweh, for He is good,
           His love is everlasting!
       Let the House of Israel say it,
           "His love is everlasting!"
Choir: Let the House of Aaron say it,
           "His love is everlasting!"
       Let those who fear Yahweh say it,
           "His love is everlasting!"
People: Hard-pressed, I invoked Yahweh,
           He heard me and came to my relief.
       With Yahweh on my side, I fear nothing:
           what can man do to me?
       With Yahweh on my side, best help of all,
           I can triumph over my enemies.
       I would rather take refuge in Yahweh
           than rely on men;
       I would rather take refuge in Yahweh
           than rely on princes.
Choir: The pagans were swarming round me,
       in the name of Yahweh I cut them down;
       they swarmed round me closer and closer,
       in the name of Yahweh I cut them down;
       they swarmed round me like bees,
       they blazed like a thorn-fire,
       in the name of Yahweh I cut them down.
Pastor: I was pressed, pressed, about to fall,
           but Yahweh came to my help;
       Yahweh is my strength and my song,
           He has been my Saviour.
People: Shouts of joy and safety
           in the tents of the virtuous:
       Yahweh's right hand is wreaking havoc,
           Yahweh's right hand is winning,
       Yahweh's right hand is wreaking havoc!

Pastor: No, I shall not die, I shall live
           to recite the deeds of Yahweh;
       though Yahweh has punished me often,
           He has not abandoned me to Death.
Choir: Open the gates of virtue to me,
           I will come in and give thanks to Yahweh.
       This is Yahweh's gateway,
           through which the virtuous may enter.
       I thank You for having heard me,
           You have been my Savior.
People: It was the stone rejected by the builders
           that proved to be the keystone;
       this is Yahweh's doing
           and it is wonderful to see.
       This is the day made memorable by Yahweh,
           what immense joy for us!
Pastor: Please, Yahweh, please save us.
       Please, Yahweh, please give us prosperity.
       Blessings on Him who comes in the name of Yahweh!
       We bless You from the house of Yahweh.
       Yahweh is God, He smiles on us.
       With branches in your hands draw up in procession
           as far as the horns of the altar.
People: You are my God, I give You thanks,
           I extol You, my God;
       I give You thanks for having heard me,
           You have been my Saviour.
       Give thanks to Yahweh, for He is good,

Psalm 114 (TJB) *(in unison)*

           A Hymn for the Passover
       When Israel came out of Egypt,
       the House of Jacob from a foreign nation,
       Judah became his sanctuary
       and Israel his domain.

       The sea fled at the sight,
       the Jordan stopped flowing,
       the mountains skipped like rams,
       and like lambs, the hills.

       Sea, what makes you run away?
       Jordan, why stop flowing?
       Why skip like rams, you mountains,
       why like lambs, you hills?

30

His love is everlasting!
Quake, earth, at the coming of your Master,
at the coming of the God of Jacob,
who turns rock into pool
flint into fountain.

The Gloria Patri

The Narration Begins

Interpreter: The wonder of the ancient mass, source for our Order of Communion worship this evening, retells the life, death, and resurrection of our Lord Jesus Christ. To anyone who listens closely, the story unfolds step by step, reaching its climax in the "resurrection appearances of Christ" in the distribution of the bread and wine of the Sacrament.

This is Maundy Thursday evening, the night in which we traditionally celebrate the upper room experience with its emphasis on the establishment of the new covenant in His body and blood under the visible sacramental elements. Normally Lutherans begin the order of worship with a Confession of Sins and Absolution. This evening we have elected to place the Confession later in the service.

If you will allow me, I would like to briefly retell the life of Christ as a demonstration of the "story line" of the worship sequence. You, as congregation, together with the officiant this evening, will supplement the story line with the time-tested versicles, hymns, and prayers of the church's setting for Holy Communion. The "historian" will trace a third line, which follows the Passover lamb from the first Passover to the upper room Communion table.

Historian: The exodus of Israel out of Egypt under Moses' leadership is dated about thirteen hundred years before the birth of Christ. The event has been commemorated annually among the Israelites and Jews through all these thirty-two hundred years since. Each year the commemoration involves rituals which symbolically rehearse the flight from Egypt and all the bitterness that has marked their history. Always, for the Israelites and the Jew, the commemoration has been a time to look back.

The commemoration celebrates the Passover. The descendants of Joseph, son of Jacob, had stayed on in Egypt after the dreadful famine years that drew them there. Several centuries passed. They became slaves in Egypt. When their situation worsened, Yahweh, God, came to Moses at the burning bush, and pressed him into service as liberator of the slaves. Pharoah refused to release the slaves until the awesome tenth plague in which the firstborn in every Egyptian household, including the palace, was found dead one morning.

Interpreter: Throughout the Old Testament times (and still in the New, for that matter), one cry has dominated the family of man:

The Kyrie

The Narration

Interpreter: God's answer to that cry is tucked away in a gentle story in His revelation and in a forlorn stable in a little Palestinian village. At least His answer begins there, for it is in the Person of the Baby of Bethlehem that the Son of God was made incarnate, born in human flesh to reconcile the Creator to His wayward creature. Angels announced the birth and hosts of angels sang the praises of God at the onset of His great plan for our salvation.

The Gloria in Excelsis   (Christmas revisited)

The Narration

Historian: The ten plagues of Egypt were designed to bring freedom to the slaves. When the doom of the last plague was announced, special instructions were also announced among the slaves. They were, among other things, to choose a male lamb, without blemish, . . . butcher it, cook it, and in the dark of that night, eat it. Blood from the lamb was to be smeared on the lintel of the door of the slaves' hovels. The angel of judgment "passed over" every house where the casements were blood-stained. To the sound of terrible weeping, liberation began the next morning as the slaves, under Moses, moved out of the land.

The Salutation

The Collect for Maundy Thursday

The Narration

Historian: The Israelites used the great Exodus event as source-point for their being. The celebration of the Passover commemorated the emotion-packed night and morning of their liberation. Each year lambs were used in the Passover meal. Every household in which people identified with the

Exodus event celebrated, sacrificed a lamb. It was a mighty memorial feast to the birth-event of a people.

Interpreter: The Child grew to maturity. About that time John the Baptist appeared on the sweep of history and the banks of the Jordan. His mission was to be hearld to the Messiah. He preached repentance and baptism. "Make a level highway for the Lord," he cried to all who came to hear him.

The Epistle   (Echoes of John the Baptist)

The Narration

Historian: Israel may have looked back when she celebrated the Passover. God looked forward in anticipation. God had a "plan of salvation" which He most carefully unfolded through the years. The plan in its totality had its own perspective. It was not by chance that a lamb was chosen nor yet that its blood was painted on the doorposts. In perspective, the lamb and the blood became "signs" (or types), which pointed to and would be fulfilled in the New Testament. (A sign is an event that carries within itself some of the reality of the event to which it points.) It is because Jesus Christ would one day give His life for the salvation of the world as the *true* Paschal Lamb, that a lamb was used and the doorways were adorned with its blood, for He would stay the judgment when His blood (that is, His vicarious death) adorned a person's heart.

The Gospel   (Jesus begins His ministry)

Glory be to Thee, O Lord.
Praise be to Thee, O Christ!

The Nicene Creed   (The Message)

The Office Hymn
Nikolaus Decius
O Lamm Gottes, unschuldig

Lamb of God, pure and holy
(Stanza 1)

The Meditation

The Offertory   (Setting his face toward Jerusalem)

Create in me a clean heart, O God, and renew a right spirit within me. Cast me not away from Thy presence, and take not Thy Holy Spirit from me. Restore unto me the joy of Thy salvation; and uphold me with Thy free spirit. Amen.

The Offering

The Prayers

The Preface

It is truly, meet, . . . thence Life also might rise again; and that He who by a tree once overcame might likewise by a tree be overcome, through Christ, our Lord;

The Narration

Historian: Every year the Passover arrived. Many people traveled to Jerusalem to celebrate it there. The temple authorities and the merchants imported lambs for the festive tables of natives and visitors alike. Each family selected its lamb on the 14th day of Nisan and kept it for the prescribed eight days of the festival. Everywhere in the city one could hear bleating. In every lull in the "Hosanna's" at the Sunday parade He heard it. In the temple that evening He opened the animal pens to a crescendo of bleating. Every bleat of every lamb became a knell for Him.

The blood of the sacrificial lambs flowed freely. The priests, connoisseurs of lambs (they must be tender, unblemished, perfect), tested their quality. But it was all routine, all superficial. The true Lamb stood in the midst of the bleating and the slaughter, and no one noticed Him.

Interpreter: When the Father's appointed time came, Jesus set out for Jerusalem. Upon arrival He commandeered a donkey and rode into the city to the great acclaim of the people. They lined the streets crying: "Hosanna, Hosanna to the Son of David. Hosanna in the highest."

Officiant: . . . through whom with angels and archangels and with all the company of heaven we laud and magnify Thy glorious name, evermore praising Thee and saying:

The Sanctus   (The triumphal entry)

People: Holy, holy, holy, ...

The Narration

Historian: On Thursday Jesus requisitioned a room to celebrate the Passover with His disciples. Preparations included baking the unleavened bread, preparing the herbs and wine, and the slaughter of a lamb large enough to feed Jesus and His twelve guests. All afternoon the lamb roasted on a crosslike spit; one branch penetrated its length, the other separated its front feet; no bone of it had been broken. The guests gathered at the appointed time. They were early; the preparation of the lamb was not completed. The savory odors permeated the house and easily found their way to the upper room.

Interpreter: On Thursday evening Jesus gathered with His disciples in the upper room. He spoke with them of many things. "I am the Vine, ye are the branches," He said. He washed the disciples' feet. Then, needing again to know the love of His Father, and burdened with His own unique burdens, He knelt in prayer to pray the great High Priestly Prayer. One of the great petitions of the prayer was that His people all might be one.

The Lord's Prayer

The Narration

Interpreter: Chief among the upper room events was the establishment of the new covenant to replace the old. Mount Sinai was done. The grace of God in Jesus Christ for the forgiveness of sins, life, and salvation replaced it. His own body and blood were given as the sign and seal of His faithfulness.

Historian: At last the cooking of the lamb was finished. The good woman of the house sent up word. Jesus and His guests gathered around the table. The Passover meal that He had desired to eat with them began. The glasses of wine were drunk; the herbs and matzos were eaten . . .

The Consecration   (Maundy Thursday)

Officiant: Our Lord Jesus Christ, the same night in which He was betrayed . . . *(pauses)*

The Narration

Historian: With His own hands Jesus moved cups and cruets, platters and plates away from the center of the table. The lamb, the sign, was set before Him. He sat in their midst, took up the meat of the lamb, blessed it, raised His eyes to God, and offered praise. The flesh of the Passover burned in His mouth as He ate it.

The Consecration

Officiant: Our Lord Jesus Christ, the same night in which He was betrayed, took bread; etc.

The Narration

Historian: Now the type, the sign, is finished. That which it had

prefigured since the days of Moses had come. The lamb had served God's purposes; now *the* Lamb would do God's will.

The Hymn   Nikolaus Decius
O Lamm Gottes, unschuldig

Lamb of God, pure and holy
(Stanza 3)

The Narration

Interpreter: Some liberties have been taken with the normal Order. It is here, just for tonight, that the Confession of Sins and Absolution are placed. Between the Confession and Absolution is the Agnus Dei, offering a quiet glimpse of the Lamb that takes away the sins of the world.

The Confession of Sins

The Agnus Dei   (Good Friday)

Officiant and People: O Christ, Thou Lamb of God, that takest away the sin of the world, have mercy upon us. O Christ, Thou Lamb of God, that takest away the sin of the world, have mercy upon us. O Christ, Thou Lamb of God, that takest away the sin of the world, grant us Thy peace. Amen.

The Absolution

The Narration

Interpreter: When the sacrifice was done, Christ was wrapped in the winding sheet and sealed in the tomb. On Easter dawn He burst forth from the tomb and showed Himself alive to His disciples and the world. Now the risen and reigning Christ, in a most unique and sacramental way, comes to us under bread and wine and declares Himself alive again.

This is the feast of victory
for our God. Alleluia!

The Distribution   (Easter)

A Hymn *(softly)*   Samuel Medley
Duke Street

I know that my Redeemer lives
(Several stanzas)

A Reading from the Farewell Discourse

John 13:33-35
John 14:1-7

A Hymn (softly)   Joseph Scriven
                                                      Friend

What a Friend we have in Jesus
(A stanza or two)

A Second Reading from the Discourse

John 15:1-17

A Hymn (softly)   John Fawcett
                                                      Boylston

Blest be the tie that binds
(Several stanzas)

The Final Reading

John 16:1-15

A Hymn (softly)   Matthew Bridges
                                                      Diademata

Crown Him with many crowns
(Stanza 5)

The Nunc Dimittis   (Response and Pledge of Life)

The Collect of Thanksgiving

The Benediction

The Recessional

Primer Thoughts for Maundy Thursday

Maundy Thursday Communion is apt to be well attended, and therefore more time is required for distribution. It is possible to provide devotional material for those who are anticipating their attendance at the table and those who have guested and wait for the blessing. The devotions (as many as the estimated time available for them) can deal with a number of subjects interposed with fitting hymn stanzas.

Suggestions:
1. A review of the Wednesday evening meditations summed up in a paragraph or two.
2. A restatement of the events of the upper room leading to the covenant and seal upon it.
3. A reexamination of the Sacrament and its purposes.
4. Statements of theologians on the Sacrament.
5. Blessings of the Sacrament (forgiveness, fellowship, presence, etc.).
6. The relation of Baptism to the Eucharist.

It takes some time to work out such a series of devotions, of course, but the educational/spiritual value of them makes the time worthwhile.

GOOD FRIDAY

Notes on Good Friday
A Tenebrae Service
Primer Thoughts for Good Friday Services
A Tre Ore Service
Primer Thoughts for Tre Ore Services

Notes on Good Friday

The day our Lord died is the most solemn day of the church year. There is no event in the long history of man that matches His crucifixion. God laid on Him "the iniquity of us all."

The crucifixion account is awful enough. In brief bold strokes the evangelists paint the picture. One can fairly "feel" the darkness. Yet what the evangelists do not say is far more terrible and terrifying. Step by relentless step Jesus, the Christ, is excised from the church, the nation, the family of man, and finally even God Himself. How else can the darkness and the rending cry from its depths be explained?

The Good Friday service presented here traces the degradation to the ultimate aloneness of the God-forsaken Christ. Such a theme demands solemnity and dignity and devotion beyond most services. The processional should be slow and majestic and silent. The readings should be done with understanding, communicating the pathos of Christ's journey to hell. The hymns, some of the church's finest, must be sung at a tempo and with a meditativeness that matches their message. Even the "relief" hymn at the end must be sung with restraint.

The climax of the service is not Christ's death. It is the cry toward the end of the darkness. It can be made climactic through the use of the organ. At the reading from Matthew 27:45-46 let the organist suggest the terror of the moment, perhaps by holding two adjacent notes in the pedals, then adding shrieking tones on the manual, increasing in fury. On the word "Me" in the Word of Jesus, the organ suddenly is silent, all lights are extinguished in the church. Nothing stirs. Then, quietly, the organist begins the melody line of the next hymn, adding the voices. The lights, enough at least to read, are returned. The moment of terror

and judgment is over. The brief meditation quietly expounds "What happened?" and the service moves on.

Death comes to Christ, but it is anticipated and merciful. There is no terror in it. "It is finished" tells us that. He commended Himself to the Father to whom He had been faithful, bowed His head and died.

The service ends with a note of peace. Reassurance has been offered, and the affirmation of hope has been made. Now only the waiting through Holy Saturday for the climax to it all: His resurrection.

A Tenebrae Service[1]

(Notes Before Beginning)

To impress on the minds and hearts of believers the awful consequences of sin and the magnitude of the Savior's sacrifice, the ancient church held a special service, called Tenebrae, in the last days of Holy Week. The word means "darkness."

It comes from the ceremony, carried out in this service, of extinguishing the candles in the "Tenebrae hearse," or sevenfold candlestand, one by one.

This service is an adaptation of the medieval Tenebrae.

The extinguishing of the candles is to remind us of the events that led to the awful darkness that covered the earth when Jesus hung on the cross.

One candle remains burning throughout the service to symbolize that even in the midst of death and darkness the forces of hell shall not prevail against the light of Christ.

His resurrection is sure.
He lives eternally.
And we, too, shall live!

Jesus, Lord,	Flogged	Alone
Betrayed	Degraded	Damned
Bound	Ridiculed	Dying
Accused	Abrogated	Dead
Excommunicated		Bruised
	Crucified	Buried
Mocked	Mocked	
Expatriated	Negated	For us.

Thank you.
Amen.

[1] The Biblical material is adapted from the King James Version.

The Choral Prelude

The Prayer

"A Service of Darkness"

Hymn by Congregation   Paul Gerhardt
(softly, meditatively, slowly)   *O Welt, sieh hier*

Upon the cross extended, See, world, thy Lord suspended, Thy Savior yields His breath. The Prince of Life from heaven Himself hath freely given To shame and blows and bitter death.

Come hither now and ponder, 'Twill fill thy soul with wonder, Blood streams from every pore. Through grief whose depth none knoweth, From His great heart there floweth Sigh after sigh of anguish o'er.

'Tis I who should be smitten, My doom should here be written: Bound hand and foot in hell. The fetters and the scourging, The floods around Thee surging, 'Tis I who have deserved them well.

The Narrator

Tonight we would like to turn time back to that first Good Friday to try to relive, in a brief hour, the emotions which those who lived it once must have had. Recall in spirit how, as the sun climbed toward it zenith that morning, they had fastened Him to the cross with great nails. At midday darkness covered the earth. At three o'clock He yielded up the ghost. Then Joseph and Nicodemus begged His body from Pontius Pilate. Quickly they took it down from the cross, and carefully they laid it to rest in the unused tomb. A watch was established, the Roman seal set on the great stone. "It is finished." O sorrow dread, God's Son is dead.

Pastor: God spared not His own Son.
People: But delivered Him up for us all.

The Choir

The Scripture Lesson   Matthew 26:47-50

The Narrator

"Judas, betrayest thou the Son of Man with a kiss?" The tragic events of that night begin, in human terms, with Judas of Kerioth. Judas was one of the Twelve, and in his twisted mind the Miracle Worker could free Himself. For thirty pieces of silver, the price of a slave, Jesus was made available to His captors.

Now Jesus is becoming the outcast One. Men have begun to turn on Him. Among men, one of His special pupils gave Him into the hands of the enemy. Is there a greater tragedy in life than to have a loved one turn to oppose?

Hymn by congregation (*) [2]   Paul Gerhardt
(softly, slowly, meditatively)   *An Wasserfluessen Babylon*

A Lamb goes uncomplaining forth, The guilt of all men bearing; And laden with the sins of earth, None else the burden sharing! Goes patient on, grows weak and faint, To slaughter led without complaint, That spotless life to offer; Bears shame, and stripes, and wounds and death, Anguish and mockery, and saith, "Willing all this I suffer."

Pastor: He is brought as a lamb to the slaughter, and as a sheep before her shearers is dumb, so He opened not His mouth. He was cut off out of the land of the living; for the transgressions of my people was He stricken.
People: He hath poured out His soul unto death, and He was numbered with the transgressors. For the transgression of my people was He stricken.

The Scripture Lesson   Matthew 26:62-68

The Narrator

Then His chosen church rejected Him. Caiaphas, the high priest, rose and tearing his garments cried out, "This Man has blasphemed God!" His church made this accusation against Him!

Can you feel the heartbreak of this? He, as God, had nourished, blessed, corrected, helped His church against countless enemies. Into her keeping He had placed the sacred trust of the promised Messiah. Now that the Messiah has come, she cries out against Him, "This Man has blasphemed God!" and makes preparations to have Him put to death.

Hymn by Congregation (*)   James Montgomery
                                                              Gethsemane

Follow to the judgment-hall, View the Lord of life arraigned; Oh, the wormwood and the gall! Oh, the pangs His soul sustained! Shun not suff'ring, shame, or loss; Learn of Him to bear the cross.

Pastor: Lament like a virgin girded with sackcloth for the husband of her youth. Howl, ye shepherds, in ashes and sackcloth; for the great and terrible day of the Lord cometh.
People: Gird yourselves and lament, ye priests. Howl, ye ministers of the altar. Come, lie all night in sackcloth.

[2] Acolyte to extinguish one candle at each asterisk.

36

The Scripture Lesson Luke 23:6-11

The Narrator

Herod would have none of Him. Herod was "the chosen people," being their titular head. But Herod mocked Him—and sent Him back to Pilate.

Has your nation ever declared you outlaw to it? Are you a man without a country? When you can feel the awful pangs of the man who has no home, you will feel what He felt that night.

Hymn by Congregation (*) Thomas Kelly
O mein Jesu, ich muss sterben

Tell me, ye who hear Him groaning, Was there ever grief like His? Friends through fear His cause disowning, Foes insulting His distress; Many hands were raised to wound Him, None would interpose to save; But the deepest stroke that pierced Him Was the stroke that Justice gave.

Ye who think of sin but lightly Nor suppose the evil great Here may view its nature rightly, Here its guilt may estimate. Mark the Sacrifice appointed, See who bears the awful load; 'Tis the Word, the Lord's Anointed, Son of Man and Son of God.

Pastor: O Jerusalem, thy dance is turned into mourning; cast up dust upon thy head and gird thee with sackcloth.

People: For thy Redeemer is cut off out of the land of the living.

The Scripture Lesson Luke 23:20-24

The Narrator

Pilate washed his hands of Him. He knew Him to be innocent, but he delivered Him to be crucified.

Pilate—the world!

The last human straw to which He could cling, the final friend to whom He could turn, His last chance of appeal, and it is gone.

Now only the Way of Sorrow lies before Him. The way of sorrow—the heavy cross, the wailing women, the taunting multitude, the bitter wine, the thorns, the nails . . . now only the cross.

The Scripture Lesson Luke 23:26-27, 32-33

Hymn by Congregation (*) Paul Gerhardt
Herzlich tut mich

O sacred Head, now wounded, With grief and shame weighed down, Now scornfully surrounded With thorns, Thine only crown. O sacred Head, what glory, What bliss, till now was Thine! Yet, though despised and gory, I joy to call Thee mine.

Men mock and taunt and jeer Thee, Thou noble countenance, Though mighty worlds shall fear Thee And flee before Thy glance! How art Thou pale with anguish, With sore abuse and scorn! How doth Thy visage languish That once was bright as morn!

Pastor: My strength is dried up like a potsherd; and my tongue cleaveth to my jaws; and thou hast brought me into the dust of death.

People: But be not Thou far from me, O Lord; O my Strength, haste Thee to help me.

The Narrator

Only once has it happened in all history. Only once has God forsaken a man, and that Man was Jesus, the Christ.

Try, but you cannot imagine what it means to be forsaken by God. Lo, He is with you always, even unto the end of the world.

That's why that cry from the cross is such an agonizing cry. This was the final depth to which He could be consigned that day on which He was our Substitute in death.

The Scripture Lesson Matthew 27:45-46

The Silent Meditation

Hymn by Congregation (*) Johann Heermann
Herzliebster Jesu

O dearest Jesus, what law hast Thou broken That such sharp sentence should on Thee be spoken? Of what great crime hast Thou to make confession—What dark transgression?

Whence come these sorrows, whence this mortal anguish? It is my sins for which Thou, Lord, must languish; Yea, all the wrath, the woe, Thou dost inherit, This I do merit.

The Brief Meditation

Hymn by Congregation (*) Author unknown
Christe, du Lamm Gottes

O Christ, Thou Lamb of God, that takest away the sin of the world, have mercy upon us!

O Christ, Thou Lamb of God, that takest away the sin of the world, have mercy upon us!

O Christ, Thou Lamb of God, that takest away the sin of the world, grant us Thy peace!

The Scripture Lesson   Luke 23:46

The Narrator

Then, when He had cried with a loud voice, He bowed His head and gave up the ghost. Forsaken by man and God in His supreme sacrifice for God and for man, He died. And when the soldiers came, they pierced His side, and forthwith came out blood and water. It is said by physicians that this is a symptom of one who has died of a broken heart.

Pastor: I am counted with them that go down into the pit; I am as a man that hath no strength, free among the dead.
People: Thou hast laid me in the lowest pit, in darkness, in the deep. I am as a man that hath no strength.

The Narrator

They took Him down from the cross, then. Gently and tenderly Joseph and Nicodemus took His body down and carried it to the unused tomb. Then, the Passover being at hand, they went to their homes to keep the ancient feast.

Sadness and gloom and sorrow filled their being. He whom they loved was dead.

Hymn by Congregation (*)   Johann Rist
                                                        O Traurigkeit

O sorrow dread! God's Son is dead! But by His expiation Of our guilt upon the cross Gained for us salvation.
O Ground of faith, Laid low in death, Sweet lips, now silent sleeping! Surely all that live must mourn Here with bitter weeping.

The Scripture Lesson   Luke 23:50-53

Pastor: When the Lord was buried, they made the sepulcher sure, rolling a great stone to the door of the sepulcher, sealing the stone and setting a watch.
People: The chief priests and Pharisees came together unto Pilate and besought him, sealing the stone and setting a watch.

The Narrator

Behold, one light still burns. They have not all gone out.

Nor have they forever taken the life of my Lord. The hellish crew, death, the grave, these shall not hold Him, for in three days He will raise up again the Temple which they sought to destroy. They are not the victor! It is He who triumphs!

In the chaos of the elements, through the quaking earth, the rending veil, the opening graves, He lives! Thousand, thousand thanks shall be, dearest Jesus, unto Thee.

Hymn by Congregation (with restraint)   Ernst C. Homburg
                                                    Jesu, meines Lebens Leben

Christ, the Life of all the living, Christ, the Death of death, our foe, Who, Thyself for me once giving To the darkest depths of woe— Through Thy suff'rings, death, and merit I eternal life inherit: Thousand, thousand thanks shall be, Dearest Jesus, unto Thee.

The Scripture Lesson   Luke 23:54-56

Pastor: But Thou, O Lord, have mercy upon us.
People: Thanks be to Thee, O Lord.
Pastor: The women sitting at the sepulcher were weeping and lamenting for the Lord. Christ became obedient unto death, even the death of the cross.
People: Wherefore God hath highly exalted Him and given Him a name which is above every name, that at the name of Jesus every knee should bow, of things in heaven and things on earth and things under the earth.
Pastor: Let us with bowed heads, and in silence, pray the Lord's Prayer. (Then)

Almighty God, we beseech Thee graciously to behold this Thy family, for which our Lord Jesus Christ was content to be betrayed and given up into the hands of wicked men and to suffer death upon the cross; through the same Jesus Christ, Thy Son, our Lord, who liveth and reigneth with Thee and the Holy Ghost, ever one God, world without end. Amen.

With heads still bowed, the congregation shall receive the Benediction.

And when all have spoken a silent prayer, let them depart in silence from this House of God.

Primer Thoughts for Good Friday Services

Good Friday has a hundred facets. A meaningful service can be shaped from almost every one of them. The cross event is profound theology. God in His most awesome wrath and God in His deepest love dominates the scene. Move over only a foot and Christ the Messiah is undisputed Protagonist. Another step and the Holy Spirit, for whom the cross is the balm for sin-troubled souls, emerges from the gloom. Just over there Satan, arch antagonist to

Christ and God, holds sway. The people, the thieves, the Words from the cross, the darkness, death, new life—all cry to be heard. The last word about Good Friday has yet to be said.

Here are some "primer thoughts" about services that might be developed.

1. A service of light

Paraphrase the Passion story with the idea in mind of bathing the chancel in symbolic color. Then use colored floods on rheostats on the chancel. Focus a white spot, controlled by a dimmer, on the cross or Christ-figure dominating the sanctuary. As the paraphrase unfolds, the nave lights are lowered; the altar is lighted in blue. At the mocking, amber light undulate, giving way at last to deep red floods to symbolize the darkness. At the end, in the peace after the quaking earth, the peaceful blues flood the area once again. Each time Christ speaks, the white spot comes to full brilliance, then recedes. Such a commemoration of the Good Friday events can be surrounded by Vespers.

2. A song service

If the choir chooses to do a special piece, say "The seven last words" or "Jesus, priceless Treasure," it is possible to put their offering and message into a setting. Why not between Confession and Absolution, thus stressing the magnitude of the effort God went to in Christ to make the words of Absolution possible?

Several themes may run through a service. Should the choir be singing "Jesus, priceless Treasure" or a selection of several Good Friday anthems, intersperse them with Isaiah 53, Romans 5 or 7, or even the Passion story itself. Albrecht Duerer's Little Passion series might run through the printed Order, if some modern reproducing equipment is available.

3. A service can be developed around Martin Buber's *I and Thou* essay title, making "I and Thou" the motif. The "I" then becomes the sinner, the "Thou" is the stern Father and Judge. Between the "I" and the "Thou" must be inserted the "He," who brings the "I" and "Thou" together into a new and reconciled relationship.

4. The Seven Words lend themselves to an hour-long service (as opposed to a Tre Ore), each Word being given a little setting of its own, each meditation in it carefully sculptured to be a fitting vehicle for the wonder of it.

5. St. Bernard's meditation on a crucifix, divided into seven parts (for the hands, feet, heart of Christ), out of which "O sacred Head" originated, makes an excellent outline for a service.

Tre Ore

A Good Friday Meditation
on
The Seven Last Words of Jesus

Prelude

Silent Meditation

. . . Jesus knew that His hour was come that He should depart out of this world unto the Father, having loved His own which were in the world, He loved them unto the end. (John 13:1)*

The Hymn of Christ's Love   William McComb
Gethsemane

Chief of sinners though I be
(Stanzas 1—4)

The Prayer

Officiant: Holy Spirit,
In unison: grant us courage to review the Passion of our Lord;
Officiant: Holy Spirit,
In unison: give us insight into the love of our Lord;
Officiant: Holy Spirit,
In unison: be present with us to bless us;
Officiant: Holy Spirit,
In unison: cover our sins with the righteousness of Jesus, and hide our souls from the vision of the Judge and give us faith.
Officiant: Holy Spirit,
In unison: hear us in Jesus' name. Amen.

The Scripture   The Servant: Isaiah 53
The Servant: John 13:4-9

V. But Thou, O Lord, have mercy upon us.
R. Thanks be to Thee, O Lord!

The Hymn (concluded)   William McComb
Gethsemane

O my Savior, help afford
(Stanza 5)

The Silent Meditation

* All Scripture in this service is King James Version.

————————————————

As the Father hath loved Me, so have I loved you; continue ye in My love. (John 15:9)

The First Word

The Scripture: And when they were come to the place which is called Calvary, there they crucified Him, and the malefactors, one on the right hand, and the other on the left. (Luke 23:33)

The Hymn   Thomas B. Pollock
Septem Verba

Jesus, in Thy dying woes

The Responsive Reading   (From Psalm 22)

V. Our father trusted in Thee: they trusted, and Thou didst deliver them.

R. But I am a worm, and no man; a reproach of men, and despised of the people.

V. All they that see Me laugh Me to scorn; they shoot out the lip, they shake the head, saying,

R. He trusted on the Lord that He would deliver Him; let Him deliver Him, seeing He delighted in Him.

V. They gaped upon Me with their mouths, as a ravening and a roaring lion.

R. I am poured out like water, and all My bones are out of joint; My heart is like wax, it is melted in the midst of my bowels.

V. For dogs have compassed Me, the assembly of the wicked have inclosed Me; they pierced My hands and My feet.

R. I may tell all my bones; they look and stare upon Me.

The Scripture: Then said Jesus, "Father, forgive them; for they know not what they do." (Luke 23:34)

The Meditation

The Prayer

The Hymn   Charlotte Elliott
Woodworth

Just as I am, without one plea
(Stanza 6)

The Silent Meditation

_____

Greater love hath no man than this, that a man lay down his life for his friends. Ye are My friends . . . (John 15:13-14)

The Second Word

The Scripture: And one of the malefactors which were hanged railed on Him, saying, "If Thou be Christ, save Thyself and us." (Luke 23:39)

The Hymn   Thomas B. Pollock
Septem Verba

Jesus, pitying the sighs

The Responsive Reading   "The Mockery at the Cross"
(Selected Scripture)

V. And the rulers also with them derided Him, saying,

R. "He saved others; let Him save Himself, if He be Christ, the chosen of God."

V. And the soldiers also mocked Him, coming to Him, and offering Him vinegar, and saying,

R. "If Thou be the King of the Jews, save Thyself."

V. And they that passed by reviled Him, wagging their heads, and saying,

R. "Thou that destroyest the temple, and buildest it in three days, save Thyself. If Thou be the Son of God, come down from the cross."

V. Likewise also the chief priests mocking Him, with the scribes and elders, said,

R. "He saved others; Himself He cannot save. . . . He trusted in God; let Him deliver Him now if He will have Him; for He said, 'I am the Son of God.'"

The Scripture: And one of the malefactors which were hanged railed on Him, saying, "If Thou be Christ, save Thyself and us." But the other answering rebuked him, saying, "Dost not thou fear God, seeing thou art in the same condemnation? And we indeed justly, for we receive the due reward of our deeds; but this Man hath done nothing amiss." And he said unto Jesus, "Lord, remember me when Thou comest into Thy kingdom." And Jesus said unto him, "Verily I say unto thee, Today shalt thou be with Me in paradise." (Luke 23:39-43)

The Meditation

The Prayer

The Hymn   Paul Gerhardt
An Wasserfluessen Babylon

A Lamb goes uncomplaining forth
(Stanza 5)

The Silent Meditation

I in them, and Thou in Me, that they may be made perfect in one; and that the world may know that Thou hast sent Me, and hast loved them as Thou hast loved Me. (John 17:23)

The Third Word

The Scripture: Now there stood by the cross of Jesus His mother and His mother's sister, Mary the wife of Cleophas, and Mary Magdalene. (John 19:25)

The Hymn   Thomas B. Pollock
Septem Verba

Jesus, loving to the end

The Responsive Reading   "Pondering All These Things"
(Selected Scripture)

V. Behold, this Child is set for the fall and rising again of many in Israel, and for a sign which shall be spoken against;
R. Yea, a sword shall pierce through thy own soul also.
V. Who is My mother, and who are My brethren?
R. And He stretched forth His hand toward His disciples and said, "Behold My mother and My brethren."
V. Peace I leave with you, My peace I give unto you; not as the world giveth, give I unto you.
R. Let not your heart be troubled, neither let it be afraid.
V. In My Father's house are many mansions.
R. I go to prepare a place for you.
V. But I am a worm and no man.
R. And an alien unto My mother's children.
V. He is brought as a lamb to the slaughter, and as a sheep before her shearers is dumb, so He opened not His mouth.
R. He was cut off out of the land of the living; for the transgression of My people was He stricken.
V. He hath poured out His soul unto death, and He was numbered with the transgressors.
R. For the transgression of My people was He stricken.
V. Behold, this Child is set for the fall and rising again of many in

Israel, and for a sign which shall be spoken against;
R. Yea, a sword shall pierce through thy own soul also.

The Scripture: When Jesus therefore saw His mother, and the disciple standing by, whom He loved, He saith unto His mother, "Woman, behold thy son!" Then saith He to the disciple, "Behold thy mother!" (John 19:26-27)

The Meditation

The Prayer

The Hymn   John Fawcett
Boylston

Blest be the tie that binds
(Stanza 4)

The Silent Meditation

The life which I now live in the flesh I live by the faith of the Son of God, who loved me and gave Himself for me. (Galatians 2:20)

The Fourth Word

The Scripture: And it was about the sixth hour, and there was a darkness over all the earth until the ninth hour. (Luke 23:44)

The Responsive Reading   "The Fearful Day of the Lord"
(Selected Scripture)

V. The sun and moon shall be darkened, and the stars shall withdraw their shining; this is the day of the Lord.
R. The Lord also shall roar out of Zion and utter His voice from Jerusalem, and the heavens and the earth shall shake.
V. Behold, the day of the Lord cometh, cruel both with wrath and fierce anger, for the stars of heaven and the constellations thereof shall not give light;
R. The sun shall be darkened in his going forth, and the moon shall not cause her light to shine.
V. I clothe the heavens with blackness,
R. And I make sackcloth their covering.
V. And it shall come to pass in that day, saith the Lord God, that I will cause the sun to go down at noon,
R. And I will darken the earth in a clear day.

The Scripture: And about the ninth hour Jesus cried with a loud voice, saying, "Eli, Eli, lama sabachthani?" that is to say, "My

God, My God, why hast Thou forsaken Me?" (Matthew 27:46)

The Meditation

The Prayer

The Responsive Reading   "Prayer from the Cross"
(From Psalm 22)

V. Be not Thou far from Me, O Lord; O My Strength, haste Thee to help Me.
R. Deliver My soul from the sword; My darling from the power of the dog.
V. Be not far from Me, for trouble is near; for there is none to help.
R. Many bulls have compassed Me; strong bulls of Bashan have beset Me round.

The Hymn   Johann Heermann
Herzliebster Jesu

O dearest Jesus, what law hast Thou broken

The Silent Meditation

———————————

Who shall separate us from the love of Christ? (Romans 8:35)

Interlude

The Scripture: Let this mind be in you, which was also in Christ Jesus, who, being in the form of God, thought it not robbery to be equal with God, but made Himself of no reputation, and took upon Him the form of a servant, and was made in the likeness of men; and being found in fashion as a man, He humbled Himself and became obedient unto death, even the death of the cross. (Philippians 2:5-8)

The Hymn   Nikolaus Decius
O Lamm Gottes, unschuldig

Lamb of God, pure and holy

The Scripture: Wherefore God also hath highly exalted Him and given Him a name which is above every name, that at the name of Jesus every knee should bow, of things in heaven and things in earth and things under the earth, and that every tongue should confess that Jesus Christ is Lord, to the glory of God the Father. (Philippians 2:9-11)

The Hymn   Paul Gerhardt
An Wasserflussen Babylon

A Lamb goes uncomplaining forth
(Stanza 6)

The Silent Meditation

———————————

Hereby perceive we the love of God, because He laid down His life for us; and we ought to lay down our lives for the brethren. (1 John 3:16)

The Fifth Word

The Scripture: After this, Jesus knowing that all things were now accomplished that the Scripture might be fulfilled, saith, "I thirst." (John 19:28)

The Hymn   Thomas B. Pollock
Septem Verba

Jesus, in Thy thirst and pain

The Responsive Reading   "From the Prayers of Christ"
(Selected Scripture)

V. My strength is dried up like a potsherd, and My tongue cleaveth to My jaws;
R. And Thou hast brought Me into the dust of death.
V. They gave Me gall for My meat;
R. And in My thirst they gave Me vinegar to drink.
V. My flesh shall rest in hope.
R. For Thou wilt not leave My soul in hell; neither wilt Thou suffer Thine Holy One to see corruption.
V. Yea, though I walk through the valley of the shadow of death,
R. I will fear no evil. For Thou art with Me; Thy rod and Thy staff, they comfort Me.

The Scripture: After this, Jesus knowing that all things were now accomplished that the Scripture might be fulfilled, saith, "I thirst." (John 19:28)
    And straightway one of them ran, and took a sponge, and filled it with vinegar, and put it on a reed, and gave Him to drink. The rest said, "Let be, let us see whether Elias will come to save Him." (Matthew 27:48-49)

The Meditation

The Prayer

The Hymn   Horatius Bonar
Vox dilecti

I heard the voice of Jesus say

The Silent Meditation

And to know the love of Christ, which passeth knowledge, that ye might be filled with all the fulness of God. (Ephesians 3:19)

The Sixth Word

The Scripture: When Jesus therefore had received the vinegar, He said, "It is finished." (John 19:30)

The Hymn   Thomas B. Pollock
Septum Verba

Jesus, all our ransom paid

The Responsive Reading   "Point and Counterpoint"
(Selected Scripture)

V. Let this mind be in you, which was also in Christ Jesus, who, being in the form of God, thought it not robbery to be equal with God.

R. God hath not appointed us to wrath, but to obtain salvation by our Lord Jesus Christ.

V. But made Himself of no reputation, and took upon Him the form of a servant, and was made in the likeness of men.

R. For such an high priest became us, who is holy, harmless, undefiled, separate from sinners, and made higher than the heavens.

V. And being found in fashion as a man, He humbled Himself and became obedient unto death, even the death of the cross.

R. But He was wounded for our transgressions, He was bruised for our iniquities: the chastisement of our peace was upon Him, and with His stripes we are healed.

The Scripture: When Jesus therefore had received the vinegar, He said, "It is finished." (John 19:30)

The Meditation

The Prayer

The Responsive Reading   "Mission Accomplished"
(Selected Scripture)

V. Our Savior Jesus Christ hath abolished death and brought life and immortality to light through the Gospel.

R. O sing unto the Lord a new song, for He hath done marvelous things; His right hand and His holy arm hath gotten Him the victory.

V. Christ blotted out the handwriting of ordinances that was against us, which was contrary to us, and took it out of the way, nailing it to His cross.

R. He hath remembered His mercy and His truth toward the house of Israel; all the ends of the earth have seen the salvation of our God.

V. Having spoiled principalities and powers, Christ made a show of them openly, triumphing over them.

R. He cometh to judge the earth, with righteousness shall He judge the world, and the people with equity.

The Hymn   Johann Franck
Jesu, meine Freude

Jesus, priceless Treasure

The Silent Meditation

And walk in love, as Christ also hath loved us, and hath given Himself for us an offering and a sacrifice to God for a sweet-smelling savor. (Ephesians 5:2)

The Seventh Word

The Scripture: And when Jesus had cried with a loud voice, He said, "Father, into Thy hands I commend My spirit"; and having said thus, He gave up the ghost. (Luke 23:46)

The Solo

The Responsive Reading   "Gems from the Upper Room"
(Selected Scripture)

V. Let not your heart be troubled; ye believe in God, believe also in Me.

R. Peace I leave with you, My peace I give unto you. Let not your heart be troubled, neither let it be afraid.

V. In My Father's house are many mansions; if it were not so, I would have told you.

R. Greater love hath no man than this, that a man lay down his life for his friends. Ye are My friends.

V. And if I go and prepare a place for you, I will come again and receive you unto Myself, that where I am, there ye may be also.

R. Father, I will that they also whom Thou hast given Me be with Me where I am, that they may behold My glory, which Thou hast given Me.

V. And whither I go ye know, and the way ye know.

R. Thomas saith unto Him, "Lord, we know not whither Thou goest, and how can we know the way?"

V. Jesus saith unto him, "I am the Way, the Truth, and the Life; no man cometh unto the Father but by Me."

R. Let not your heart be troubled; ye believe in God, believe also in Me.

The Hymn   Thomas B. Pollock
Septem Verba

Jesus, all thy labor vast

The Scripture: And when Jesus had cried with a loud voice, He said, "Father, into Thy hands I commend My spirit"; and having said thus, He gave up the ghost. (Luke 23:46)

The Meditation

The Prayer

The Silent Meditation

For God so loved the world that He gave His only begotten Son, that whosoever believeth in Him should not perish but have everlasting life. (John 3:16)

Postlude

The Scripture: Jesus, when He had cried again with a loud voice, yielded up the ghost. And behold, the veil of the temple was rent in twain from the top to the bottom, and the earth did quake, and the rocks rent, and the graves were opened; and many bodies of the saints which slept arose, and came out of the graves after His resurrection, and went into the holy city, and appeared unto many. Now when the centurion and they that were with him, watching Jesus, saw the earthquake and those things that were done, they feared greatly, saying, "Truly this was the Son of God." (Matthew 27:50-54)

The Hymn   Paul Gerhardt
Herzlich tut mich

O sacred Head, now wounded
(Stanza 8)

The Responsive Reading   "The Last Word"
(Selected Scripture)

V. All they that see Me laugh Me to scorn; they shoot out their lip, they shake their head.

R. He that sitteth in the heavens shall laugh; the Lord shall have them in derision.

V. The wicked plotteth against the just and gnasheth upon him with his teeth.

R. The Lord shall laugh at him, for He seeth that his day hath come.

V. Behold, they belch out with their mouth; swords are in their lips; for who, say they, doth hear?

R. But Thou, O Lord, shalt laugh at them; Thou shalt have all the heathen in derision.

V. This is My beloved Son, in whom I am well pleased.

R. Wherefore God hath highly exalted Him and given Him a name which is above every name, that at the name of Jesus every knee should bow, of things in heaven and things in earth and things under the earth.

V. Glory be to the Father and to the Son and to the Holy Ghost.

R. As it was in the beginning, is now, and ever shall be, world without end. Amen.

The Solo

The Scripture: When the even was come, there came a rich man of Arimathea, named Joseph, who also himself was Jesus' disciple. He went to Pilate and begged the body of Jesus. Then Pilate commanded the body to be delivered. And when Joseph had taken the body, he wrapped it in a clean linen cloth and laid it in his own new tomb, which he had hewn out in the rock; and he rolled a great stone to the door of the sepulchre, and departed. And there was Mary Magdelene, and the other Mary, sitting over against the sepulchre." (Matthew 27:57-61)

The Prayer

The Hymn

Christian F. Gellert
Jesus, meine Zuversicht

Jesus lives! The victory's won!
(Stanza 4)

The Benediction

The Silent Worship

Suggested Time Sequence

Prelude	12:00—12:10
First Word	12:10—12:32
Second Word	12:32—12:54
Third Word	12:54—1:16
Fourth Word	1:16—1:38
Fifth Word	1:38—2:00
Sixth Word	2:00—2:22
Seventh Word	2:22—2:44
Postlude	2:44—3:00

Primer Thoughts for Tre Ore Services

Although the Tre Ore most frequently examines and celebrates the seven words of Christ from the cross, other themes can be developed without destroying the Tre Ore concept and message or the Tre Ore mood. There is nothing sacred about the number seven. The service can be divided into six or three or ten parts. The divisions do give opportunity for those who come for only a portion of the service to slip in or out. They provide for a little stirring space for the congregation and a motion place for the participating preachers. A few primer thoughts for other developments are in order.

1. The "If's" of the Passion story ("If these things be done in a green tree . . .").
2. A selection of the stations of the cross.
3. Christ outlawed (as suggested in the accompanying Good Friday service).
4. Studies of the people on Golgotha as they affect and react to Christ.
5. A study of the "enemies" defeated by the cross.
6. A review of the canonical hours in a series of miniatures.
7. The cross at the center of history (Fall, prophecy, event, effect).

EASTER

Notes on Easter Sunrise
A Sunrise Service
Easter Celebration Notes
Primer Thoughts for Easter

Notes on Easter Sunrise

Easter is a great day on which to meet the dawn! As once the women hastened toward the tomb in the long, low rays of the rising sun, so contemporary Christians can, on an Easter morning, gather at the holy day's beginning to greet their reigning and ruling Lord.

The morning service offers some interesting possibilities. If the "Alleluia" banner was "buried" on Ash Wednesday, it may be the first note of the service to mark the Lord's resurrection as it is carried triumphantly to its special place near the altar. Other joyous banners may follow. If the worshipers are seated outside facing east, make banners of translucent material so the rising sun lights them. A lily-covered cross made from the Christmas tree is a fine focal point. Trumpets, choirs, ensembles of available instruments, whatever the community contains, bring breadth and excitement to the service.

The length of the service (and the meditation) must fit the moment and community. The Benediction may be left unsaid, suggesting that the worship for the day is not really over. Breakfast, when space and time are available, offers opportunity for fellowship on the Lord's special day.

In the service presented here, two three-inch-thick plywood boxes, built to resemble a broken sarcophagus lid, formed the focal point. The pieces were carried in by several young men. They were placed high enough that the worshipers could see them. To the medieval mind the broken lid suggested the breaking of the binding power of the Law at Calvary and Christ's victory over it. The responsive reading seeks to emphasize the triumph of the Gospel.

Christ lives! We live! Alleluia!

Preservice Input

Medieval art was greatly circumscribed, but the end result helped the illiterate peasant to recognize who and what the artist was depicting. For instance, in spite of the "cave in the garden" as the Bible has it, Jesus is often shown emerging from a sarcophagus. The lid is shoved aside and Jesus, holding a pennon or a banner, is poised with His foot on it. Symbolically the tomb lid stood for the law of Moses, which in and through Christ has been abrogated, giving man, by his choice of Christ, a new freedom in Christ from those evil elements of life which Christ came to destroy. The broken lid is symbol for a little while at our sunrise service this year.

A Sunrise Service

The Feast of Easter

Christ is risen!
He is risen indeed!
Alleluia!

The Order of Worship

The Prelude

The Symbol   Posting the Alleluia Banner

(The "Alleluia" banner, buried on Ash Wednesday, or the First Sunday in Lent, carried into the assembly at the outset of the first service on Easter.)

The Processional   Author unknown
Gelobt sei Gott

Ye sons and daughters of the King

An Act of Worship

Pastor: Alleluia!
People: Alleluia! Alleluia!
Pastor: This is the day which the Lord hath made!
People: Alleluia!
Pastor: We will rejoice and be glad in it!
People: Alleluia!
Pastor: This is the feast of victory for our God!
People: Alleluia!
Pastor: The Lamb of God lives and reigns!
People: Alleluia!
Pastor: The Son of God sits high and exalted on His eternal throne!

People: Alleluia!
Pastor: This is the feast of victory for our God!
People: Alleluia!

The Easter Story   The Gospel of St. Mark 16:1-8

The Anthem

The Epistle   Romans 5:12-21

A Responsive Reading   (KJV, NEB)

Pastor: "Thou shalt have no other gods before Me." (Ex. 20:3)
People: "He rescued us from the domain of darkness and brought us away into the kingdom of His dear Son, in whom our release is secured and our sins forgiven." (Col. 1:13-14)
Pastor: "Thou shalt not take the name of the Lord thy God in vain . . ." (Ex. 20:7)
People: "For all who are moved by the Spirit of God are sons of God. The Spirit you have received is not a spirit of slavery leading you back into a life of fear, but a Spirit that makes us sons, enabling us to cry 'Abba! Father!'" (Rom. 8:14-15)
Pastor: "Remember the sabbath day, to keep it holy." (Ex. 20:8)
People: I became the servant of the church . . . "to deliver [God's] message in full; to announce the secret hidden for long ages. . . . The secret is this: Christ in you, the hope of a glory to come." (Col. 1:25-27)
Pastor: "Honor thy father and thy mother: that thy days may be long upon the land which the Lord thy God giveth thee." (Ex. 20:12)
People: "For it is in Christ that the complete Being of the Godhead dwells embodied, and in Him you have been brought to completion. Every power and authority in the universe is subject to Him as Head." (Col. 2:9-10)
Pastor: "Thou shalt not kill." (Ex. 20:13)
People: "Therefore, my brothers, I implore you by God's mercy to offer your very selves to Him: a living sacrifice, dedicated and fit for His acceptance, the worship offered by mind and heart." (Rom. 12:1)
Pastor: "Thou shalt not commit adultery." (Ex. 20:14)
People: ". . . the harvest of the Spirit is love, joy, peace, patience, kindness, goodness, fidelity, gentleness, and self-control. There is no law dealing with such things as these." (Gal. 5:22-23)
Pastor: "Thou shalt not steal." (Ex. 20:15)

People: ". . . you know how generous our Lord Jesus Christ has been: He was rich, yet for your sake He became poor, so that through His poverty you might become rich." (2 Cor. 8:9)

Pastor: "Thou shalt not bear false witness against thy neighbor." (Ex. 20:16)

People: "There is one body and one Spirit, as there is also one hope held out in God's call to you; one Lord, one faith, one baptism; one God and Father of all, who is over all and through and in all." (Eph. 4:4-6)

Pastor: "Thou shalt not covet . . . ." (Ex. 20:17)

People: "He it is who sacrificed Himself for us, to set us free from all wickedness and to make us a pure people marked out for His own, eager to do good." (Titus 2:14)

Pastor: "Drive out the slave-woman and her son, for the son of the slave shall not share the inheritance with the free woman's son." (Gal. 4:30)

People: " . . . we are no slave-woman's children; our mother is the free woman. Christ set us free, to be free men." (Gal. 4:31—5:1)

Pastor: Christ is risen.

People: He is risen indeed.

The Hymn   William B. Collyer
                                              Innocents

Morning breaks upon the tomb

The Message

The Offering

The Prayers

The Benediction

The Recessional   Author unknown
                                              Easter Hymn

Jesus Christ is ris'n today, Alleluia!

Easter Celebration Notes

The salesman with the little four-rank organ tells his customer not to pull all the stops at once. If the organist needs something extra from his little four ranks, he does well to save a stop until then. Easter is the day for "full organ." The big planning and the something extra belong to the big day. Easter is THE day of the Christian church, exceeded by no other day, for the resurrection of Christ from the dead and its implications for us are superseded by no other fact of human history.

On the feast of Easter every Christian community must by necessity use its own "stops." Its offering ought to be most uniquely the community's own. From the pastor who makes the proclamation, through the organist and choir, the altar guild and banner-makers, all the way to the custodian, everyone ought to present his extra best to the Christ who is Lord.

At the same time something of the community's usual formula for worship ought to be in evidence for the sake of the visitor or the "Easter Christians" in the community. The continuing and the familiar can be as important and certainly as valid on Easter as the extra stop or two saved for this exciting feast.

No Easter worship service is presented in this collection of services. The "Primer" thoughts may offer some suggestions that could be used to embellish and vary the normal Sunday Order without violating it with drastic change.

It is well to keep in mind that as Christmas celebrated "Light" in the dark and dismal season of the year (and the soul), so Easter celebrates "Life" in the time of the year's awakening. Somehow, the glory of "life" must dominate worship on the day of the Lord's resurrection. But then, how could that be missed!

Primer Thoughts for Easter

1. Variations on the Easter Theme
The Easter service may be introduced with the choir singing from the narthex:

1. Palm Sunday remembered
   Ride on, ride on, in majesty!
   In lowly pomp ride on to die.

and a solo voice from the gallery:

2. Good Friday recalled
   O sorrow dread!
   God's Son is dead!

and a moment of silence

3. Holy Saturday restated
   A moment of silence
   after which the service begins.

2. The Victory Theme of Easter might be stated just before the Greater Gloria:

A Responsive Reading   Selected Scripture Readings

I
The Victory Over Sin

All have sinned and come short of the glory of God: There is not a just man upon earth that doeth good and sinneth not.

All we like sheep have gone astray: The Lord has laid on Him the iniquity of us all.

God was in Christ, reconciling the world unto Himself: Christ has blotted out the handwriting of ordinances that was against us.

Even when we were dead in sin: God has quickened us together with Christ.

This is the feast of victory for our God: Alleluia! Alleluia!

II
The Victory Over Death

Christ died for our sins and was buried: He rose again the third day. Alleluia! Alleluia!

If Christ is not raised your faith is vain: But now is Christ risen.

O Death, where is thy sting?: O Grave, where is thy victory?

Thanks be to God which giveth us the victory through our Lord Jesus Christ: Now is Christ risen and become the firstfruits of them that sleep.

This is the feast of victory for our God: Alleluia! Alleluia!

III
The Victory over Satan

Be sober, be vigilant: Your adversary the devil, as a roaring lion, walketh about, seeking whom he may devour.

Now is the judgment of this world: Now shall the prince of this world be cast out.

Christ also Himself likewise put on our flesh and blood: That through death He might destroy Him that had the power of death, that is, the devil.

Christ our Lord spoiled principalities and powers: He made a show of them openly, triumphing over them.

This is the feast of victory for our God: Alleluia! Alleluia!

Epilog
The Victor

God has raised His Christ from the dead: He has set Him at His own right hand in the heavenly places.

He reigns above all principality and power and might and dominion: And every name that is named,

Not only in this world: But also in that which is to come.

God has put all things under His feet: And has made Him to be Head over all things.

This is the feast of victory for our God: Alleluia! Alleluia!

3. The Apostles' Creed (or Nicene) may be interrupted at the words: "The third day he rose again from the dead." The service now continues, working out the implications of that affirmation of the Creed, with the Office of the Word, the joyous anthems, the sermon and the prayers. Before the service ends, the Creed, picked up where it had been interrupted, is concluded.

4. Psalm 24 was used by the church in the Middle Ages not only at Christmas but at Easter. Originally it was written for the entrance of the Ark of the Covenant into the Holy City and the Temple. That alone gives the Psalm all kinds of excitement. It was natural for Christians to use it for Christmas, the celebration of the entrance of the Son of God into our world. Its use at Easter suggests some exciting ideas. The Psalm may be read at the outset. The opening verses call for Confession and Absolution. Interrupt the reading for that, then finish the Psalm.

   Christ's descent into hell, His return to the "land of the living," His ascent into glory, and His advent into people's hearts are suggestions as to why "the gates should lift up their heads." The last verses of the Psalm might conclude the service, sending the worshipers back to the world with the Good News ringing in their ears and Christ alive and well in their lives.

5. Remembering the fine practice of the church in times past and in some places of Confession and Absolution happening outside the church building, that the worshipers might come into God's house "with clean hands and holy heart," it is possible to do the Absolution before the procession or opening hymn. This allows the service to open on a paean of praise and a shout of triumph with fine justification.

ASCENSION DAY

Notes on Ascension Day
An Ascension Day Service
Primer Thoughts for Ascension Day

Notes on Ascension Day

Good Friday is heavy with pathos; Easter is buoyant with joy; Ascension is packed with wondering awe. Each celebration has its special reason for being and its own built-in excitement. Ascension, with its heaven-side/earth-side involvements, offers an excellent opportunity to speak of the mighty sacramental activity of God and His Christ and at the same time gives ample opportunity to respond in sacrificial praise and thanksgiving and in new determination "to live under Him in His kingdom and serve Him."

Not every service has to have a sermon. Sometimes it is possible to borrow a message and bend it to the theme. Here is an attempt to work out such a progression. Paragraphs and short essays were gleaned from here and there to fit the development. They were read by various people primed for the purpose. But every service ought to have a theme. Here the "King" theme is used from Christ the King's birth to His "sitting at the right hand of God," from whence He comes to live in us. Using the old Latin terms for divisions seems to add to the cohesion.

An Ascension Day Service

Notes for Appreciation

Our worship tonight uses the "Rex" (King) theme that is so strong in the Savior's life. The "King" concept somehow seems to climax in the Ascension event. This service came together when the aspects of Christ's kingship emerged in the preparation.

Christ begins His earthly life as the King of Peace, lying in a lowly manger. Through His youth and manhood His kingship is concealed. It emerges at last before Pilate. He is hung on the wood of the cross, crowned with thorns, but King He is, indeed. At Easter dawn He

assumes His kingly prerogatives. On the day of Ascension He moves in stately procession to the right hand of God the Father Almighty, from whence He shall come to judge the quick and the dead.

The "sermon" for this evening is borrowed from various preachers who seemed to say what needed to be said with deeper wisdom and better words than we would have said ti. They serve to give their own dimension to the thought of the moment.

The movement within the service is logical, coming at last to center in the Christ of the Eucharist.

The Feast of the Ascension

The Order of Worship

The Prelude

The Processional Hymn	Author unknown
	St. Agnes

O Jesus, King most wonderful

A Prayer

A Lesson	1 Corinthians 15:1-11

Recapitulation
Rex Pacificus[1]

The Hymn	Liturgy of St. James
	Picardy

Let all mortal flesh keep silence

A Reading	"The Unveiling of God"

The advent of Jesus is more than a date—it is an event; not simply an incident, but an era: it is the unveiling of God and humanity. The long periods—B.C. and A.D.—are the "folding doors of history," when prophecy was fulfilled. The time and place and persons involved in this story are all of deep significance to us, and the question that the wise men came asking, "Where is he?" is the deepest question of the ages.[2]

Our Christmas Prayer (together)

Pastor: We pray . . .
People: Eternal Father, whose Christmas presence is the best of all gifts: for the quiet Word of Bethlehem, for the loving Word in

[1] King of Peace

[2] From *Worship Resources for the Christian Year*. Reprinted by permission of Harper & Row, Publishers.

ministry, for the mighty Word of Calvary, for the affirming Word of Easter, and for the redeeming Word that fills us and causes us to glorify and praise You on this day of celebration—we thank You. Amen.

Rex Absconditus[3]

A Moment of Silence

A Prayer for the Ministry of Christ

Pastor: We pray . . .
People: All knowing, all powerful Lord, from whom come our most treasured gifts, we thank You for the Word, the Light, and the Life You have given us, and pray Your blessing to enable us to hear Him, follow Him, and live for Him in this world; through Jesus Christ, who with You and the Spirit are one eternal Godhead. Amen.

A Lesson   Luke 9:51-62

A Reading

Here is a young man who was born in an obscure village, the child of a peasant woman. He grew up in another village. He worked in a carpenter shop until He was thirty, and then for three years He was an itinerant preacher. He never wrote a book. He never held an office. He never owned a home. He never had a family. He never went to college. He never put His foot inside a big city. He never traveled 200 miles from the place where He was born. He never did one of the things that usually accompany greatness. He had no credentials but Himself.

While He was still a young man, the tide of public opinion turned against Him. His friends ran away. He was turned over to His enemies. He went through the mockery of a trial. He was nailed to the cross between two theives. While He was dying, His executioners gambled for the only piece of property He had on earth, and that was His coat. When He was dead, He was laid in a borrowed grave through the pity of a friend.

Nineteen centuries have come and gone, and today He is the central figure of the human race and the leader of the column of progress. I am far within the mark when I say that all the armies that ever marched, and all the navies that ever sailed, and all the parliaments that ever sat, and all the kings that ever reigned, put together, have not affected the life of man upon this earth as has that One Solitary Life.[4]

[3] The King concealed

[4] "One Solitary Life," author unknown.

A Hymn   Cecil F. Alexander
                                                                          Stuttgart

Jesus calls us; o'er the tumult

Regnavit a Ligno Deus[5]

A Silence

A Reading   "The Sign of the Cross"
                                                                  Herschel H. Hobbs

How varied are the views men have of the Cross! To many, it is but an ornament to be worn about the neck. To the architect it is a symbol, adorning churches. To the scholar it is a goad, driving him on in intellectual pursuits. To the preacher it is a sermon, filling the need of the hour—and of eternity. To the skeptic it is a superstition, clouding men's souls. To the Communist it is a narcotic, benumbing men's minds, an opiate of the people. To the Roman it was an instrument of execution, obnoxious and hated. To Constantine it was a sign in which to conquer, turning defeat into victory. To Paul it was a symbol of glory, pointing the way to heaven. To Mary it was a memory of agony, piercing her soul. To the Sanhedrin it was a token of victory, imaginary and short-lived. To the motley mob on Golgotha it was a holiday, carnal and cursed. To one thief it was the door to perdition, horrible and eternal. To the other it was the gate to Paradise, wondrous beyond work of men or angels. To Christ it was a bier and a throne, paradox of time, predestined to eternity. To multiplied millions of storm-tossed souls it is an anchor, offering a haven of rest.[6]

A Hymn   John Ellerton
                                                                       Gethsemane

Throned upon the awe-full tree

Rex Gloriae[7]

A Silence

A Reading   "The Glories of Easter Morn"
                                                                  George Matheson

Easter Day was a new Christmas Day; it was the second birth of Christ. His second birth was grander than his first. His first birth was

[5] God reigns from the wood of the cross

[6] From *Worship Resources for the Christian Year.* Reprinted by permission of Harper & Row, Publishers.

[7] King of Glory

under disadvantages. The disadvantages lay not in the manger, but in the royal lineage. The swaddling bands that circumscribed him were not the facts of his poverty, but the glories of his ancestors; the royal line of David separated him from the main line of humanity. But when he came from the dead he changed his lineage. He broke with the line of David—with all lines but the lowliest. His second life was not from Bethlehem: it was from the common dust of all cities—from the city of the dead. We think of him as nearer to us when a child. That is a great mistake. As a child he was always the Jewish Messiah—nearer to the tribes of Israel than to the tribes of Man. But with Easter morn he came up from the *depths*—from the dust of death. He came from the place where all join hands; and that is the secret of his resurrection power. We all meet in the lowest valley. We do not all meet on the highest mountain, on any mountain. We are not made one by joy; the privilege of the Jew divides him from the Gentile. But calamity makes us one; sin and death make us one. Christmas morning was beautiful, but it came from the fields of gold; Easter morning is more precious, for it comes from the miry clay.[8]

A Responsive Reading   Psalm 24:7-10 KJV

> *Pastor:* Lift up your heads, O ye gates; and be ye lift up, ye everlasting doors:
> *People:* And the King of Glory shall come in.
> *Pastor:* Who is this King of Glory?
> *People:* The Lord strong and mighty, the Lord mighty in battle.
> *Pastor:* Lift up your heads, O ye gates; even lift them up, ye everlasting doors:
> *People:* And the King of Glory shall come in.
> *Pastor:* Who is this King of Glory?
> *People:* The Lord of Hosts, He is the King of Glory.

A Hymn   Matthew Bridges
Diademata

Crown Him with many crowns
(Stanza 4)

A Prayer

> *Pastor:* We pray . . .
> *People:* Holy Spirit, keep us faithful to the Christ, that dying we may come to glory, and that being in glory we may be present at the majestic moment when the Son presents the kingdom of grace to His Father amid the mighty chorus of all the

[8] From *Worship Resources for the Christian Year*. Reprinted by permission of Harper & Row, Publishers.

heavenly hosts; through Jesus Christ, the Father, and You, who have effected our salvation and assured our eternity with You in the mansions. Amen.

Celebration
Christus Rex[9]

A Silence

The Ascension Gospel   Luke 24:44-53

An Ascension Hymn   Thomas Kelly
Coronae

Look, ye saints, the sight is glorious

The Lesson   Acts 1:10-14

Participation

The Sacrament of the Altar

The Waiting

1. With Prayer and Supplication
2. In Confession and Absolution
3. In the Breaking of Bread

The Distribution Hymn   Friedrich Funcke
Ach Gott und Herr

Draw us to Thee

The Lesson   1 John 4:7-11

The Prayer (in fellowship)

> *Pastor:* We pray . . .
> *People:* Holy Spirit, by whose power alone faith and sanctification are generated and sustained, move us who are the church from faith to love to unity, that the Christian community be the example of love-in-action in the world for the sake of Jesus Christ, who with You and the Father reign and rule over us forever. Amen.

The Benediction

The Recessional   Johann M. Meyfart
Jerusalem, du hochgebaute Stadt

Jerusalem, thou city fair and high

[9] Christ the King

Primer Thoughts for Ascension Day

Ascension Day services can develop around other ideas. Christ's earthly life is over. His life lends itself to review through the great hymns of the church for the seasons and through the anthems the choir has sung through the year. But more, it can be an opportunity to explore heaven through Scripture and the hymns, or the presence of Christ in us, made possible by the removal of His visible presence from among us.

1. A service outline: *This Is Your Life*, or *This Is His Life*. Develop a continuity starting with the announcement of Your/His coming; His birth, His ministry, His approaching death, His sacrifice, His resurrection, His ascension, the purpose of the Ascension, our response to it. The number of parts is expandable depending on time, choir preparation, and organist.

2. It is possible, with a series of carefully chosen Scripture passages, to build up power-charged worshipers. Such a series can be built around "The Master Plan," as suggested in Phillips' translation of the New Testament (Eph. 3). The passages are read slowly and deliberately, with a brief silence between them. The reading is broken with an interspersed hymn. Here is such a set of passages. Phillips' translation is recommended. Printing out the passages and hymns is a great help.

The Master Plan   Ephesians 3:14a
    Colossians 1:15-20
    Ephesians 1:22-23
    Philippians 2:9-11
    Hebrews 1:1-4
    Hebrews 2:8
    1 Peter 1:21
Hymn: Ye watchers and ye holy ones (St. 1)
    Colossians 3:1-4
    Ephesians 1:9-14
Hymn: O higher than the cherubim (St. 2)
    2 Thessalonians 1:7-12
    1 Timothy 6:13-16
    Revelation 12:10a
    Revelation 11:14-15

Hymn: Respond, ye souls in endless rest (St. 3)
    Revelation 15:3-4
    Revelation 4:8b-11
    Revelation 5:11-13
    1 Corinthians 15:28
    1 Timothy 1:17
Hymn: O friends, in gladness let us sing (St. 4)

The message at such a service can well center around "Time and the Master Plan," tracing the meticulous care God has exercised in planning the work of redemption, then working His plan, its first great climax in the Ascension, and the final exultant climax in Christ's return to carry His own triumphantly into glory. The worshiper is, of course, caught up in this plan. (A suggested text, at least according to Phillips, is Eph. 3:14a.)

3. An idea similar to "The Master Plan" suggested above lends itself exceedingly well to Ascension Day. The general theme is "The Indwelling Godhead." The concept is incomprehensible, appropriated only by faith and trust in the Word, but it is certainly reiterated enough times by the Spirit to make it a way by which to live! The concept lends itself to this festival because Christ can come to all of us only after His bodily presence is removed and He can exercise what the systematicians call His *illocal* presence. Here is the set of passages (again, Phillips' paraphrase reads best):

The Indwelling Godhead
The Father in Us
    1 Corinthians 6:17
    Colossians 2:10
    2 Corinthians 6:16
    John 14:23
The Hymn: Jesus, Thy boundless love to me (St. 1)
Christ in Us
    Revelation 3:20
    John 14:20
    Galatians 3:11
    Colossians 1:25-27
    Colossians 2:14
The Hymn: Oh, grant that nothing in my soul (St. 2)
The Holy Spirit in Us
    John 14:15-17
    2 Timothy 1:14
    1 Corinthians 3:16
    1 Corinthians 6:19
    Romans 8:9-11

The Hymn This love unwearied I pursue (St. 4)
A Prayer
> Ephesians 3:14-19

The Hymn: Still let Thy love point out my way (St. 6)

The idea which suggests itself for the message in this context is St. Paul's development of the *mysterion*, the mystery of Christ in us, Colossians 1:25-27 Phillips. Someone has suggested that to grasp the breadth of this whole concept one ought to memorize the Gospel of St. John.

PENTECOST

Notes on Pentecost
Countdown to Pentecost
A Pentecost Service
Primer Thoughts for Pentecost

Notes on Pentecost

Pentecost brings the Easter season to a second climax. It is not an independent feast but the seal on the Easter celebration. As Christmas and Epiphany go hand in hand, so also do these two great festivals celebrating the mighty acts of the blessed Trinity.

The church might be said to have been conceived at Caesarea Philippi in the remarkable confession of St. Peter (Matthew 16:16). Pentecost is the birthday of the church. It is the day on which the Gospel was first proclaimed in the Spirit's power and on which the church's expansion began.

Pentecost marks the beginning of the special activity of the Holy Spirit: the incessant calling, gathering, enlightening, and sanctifying in which He engages to prepare the bride for her Bridegroom. To effect faith in Christ, He uses the Word and Sacraments as channels to those in whom He elects to dwell.

The church exists only by the presence of the Spirit in it. He brings the forgiveness merited by Christ's death: ". . . 'Receive the Holy Spirit. If you forgive the sins of any, they are forgiven; . . . .'" (John 20:22-23). He speaks through the words of the preacher. He is present in the Sacrament.

Scripture teaches that the Spirit gave gifts to Jesse's Son and gives gifts to us. The gifts are symbolized here in a Pentecost countdown series of interludes in which candles are lit to individualize the gifts. The seventh candle is lit on Pentecost itself, thus joining the two festivals of life with light. The service suggested here places emphasis on the fruits of the Spirit, which ought to be the envy and petition of all Christians.

Interlude

Countdown to Pentecost (VII)
Gifts of the Holy Spirit, Isaiah 11:2

Wisdom

The church speaks of seven gifts of the Holy Spirit. In Isaiah 11:2-3 seven gifts are mentioned, but in the original the last two are repeated. The Septuagint, a translation before Christ from Hebrew to Greek, rendered one of the two phrases ("fear of the Lord") with "piety," a justifiable translation, thus making the seven gifts. The gifts are first promised to the Rod of Jesse, the Messiah. Joel 2:28 advances the distribution of the gifts to all God's people in the coming Messianic age. These sevenfold gifts of the Holy Spirit will be brought to the level of visibility and symbolized in a "Countdown to Pentecost" with a series of candles, one to be lit each Sunday for one gift. A brief interlude in the midst of the service serves as setting.

The first gift of the Spirit is "wisdom." The Greek word *sophia* means wisdom. Long ago it was decided that God alone has wisdom and that men could only be lovers of wisdom. Hence the Greek word *philosophos* and our word, "philosophy." God is "omniscient." Christ in His deity participated in God's omniscience. In the upper room Christ gave His disciples and us the secret of the deepest wisdom, "If ye continue in My Word . . . ye shall know the truth and the truth shall make you free" (John 8:31-32 KJV). It is the choicest priority and the highest wisdom to seek the truth of Christ, the truth in Christ, and the freedom of Christ. Such wisdom is indeed the gift of the Spirit.

A Hymn William W. How
Munich

O Word of God Incarnate
(Selected stanzas)

A "Wisdom" candle is lighted

The Scripture Joel 2:28-32

A Collect

Holy Spirit, who brooded over the deep at the beginning of time, and who will present the holy church as bride to Christ at the end-time, give us the wisdom to continue in the Word of Christ, thus to share in the unfolding of the divine plan in time and to behold the face of God in eternity; through Jesus Christ our Lord, with You and the Father, one God, with dominion over us forever. Amen.

The Hymn concluded William W. How
Munich

O Word of God Incarnate
(Selected stanzas)

Interlude

Countdown to Pentecost (VI)
Gifts of the Holy Spirit, Isaiah 11:2

Understanding

Youth takes a clock apart in order to "understand" it. Einstein developed his $E=MC^2$ equation in order to understand the nature of light and energy. Understanding "how's" and "why's" about little things and enormous events is basic to our living. "Being from Missouri" has its own rewards! In the list of gifts of the Spirit is understanding. Here the connotations must of necessity become spiritual. The Wisdom Literature gives an insight into this gift in Proverbs (28:5 KJV): "They that seek the Lord understand all things." When applied to the Messiah (Branch of Jesse's root, Isaiah 11:1), understanding is readily understood, for Christ and His Father are in perfect "understanding" in the councils of the Trinity. For the Christian the Trinity is the most important object of understanding. While he cannot know the deep mysteries of the triune God, he can know the divine plan for his salvation in time and his translation into eternity. In Christ the gift of such understanding, i.e., contact with God, is uniquely given to us.

A Hymn Andrew Reed
Light Divine

Holy Ghost, with light divine
(Selected stanzas)

The "Understanding" candle is lit

The Scripture 1 Corinthians 12:6-11

The Collect

Holy Spirit, to whom belongs the work of sanctification and by whom we are established in our relationship to God the Father, feed us daily with the blessed Word of our Lord's self-disclosure and allow us to drink deeply of its spring and of Christ, the Water of Life, that our understanding strengthen our faith and our faith carry us past death and over to eternal life; through Jesus Christ our Lord, with You and the Father, one God, with dominion over us forever. Amen.

The Hymn concluded   Andrew Reed
                                                        Light Divine

Holy Ghost, with light divine
(Selected stanzas)

Interlude

Countdown to Pentecost (V)
Gifts of the Holy Spirit, Isaiah 11:2

Counsel

Nowadays we take all the advice (counsel) we can find. We sift it and sort it, finally doing what the weight of all the counsel and our own psyche suggests as the best course in our dilemma. The old Hebraic idea was to ask for counsel, then to act upon it, for to ask and act otherwise was to shame the counsel and the counselor. The Old Testament idea assumes greater importance in relation to the prophets who spoke for God. To spurn the prophet's counsel was to shame God.

Early in his scroll (9:6) Isaiah had said that the name of Christ should be Counselor. In 11:2 Isaiah strengthens this prophecy as he foretells the outpouring of the gifts of the Spirit on the Messiah Christ: "The Spirit of the Lord shall rest upon Him . . . the spirit of counsel . . . ." In the Old Testament sense and therefore in the Bible sense, the advice, the counsel of Christ, ought to be accepted, lest Christ be shamed. "Repent and believe," He said. "I am the Resurrection and the Life," He said.

In secular things we retain the right in our present concept of counsel to reject or accept what our counselor offers us. In a spiritual sense, when the counsel is of God, we ought indeed to accept it. We may offer counsel to our peers in secular things, knowing it is rejectable. We may offer spiritual counsel and be forced to turn the other cheek. Yet in and through Christ we have the privilege and responsibility of offering counsel, for it is one of the gifts of the Holy Spirit to us.

The Hymn   Author Unknown
                                                        Italian Hymn

Come, Holy Ghost, in love
(Selected stanzas)

The "Counsel" candle is lit

The Scripture   Romans 12:5-7

The Collect

Holy Spirit of the blessed Trinity, whose Word is truth and whose counsel is always perfect, give us grace to translate the counsel of our God into action in our lives by believing in Christ, by trusting in the faith, and by living out our lives in accordance with the expectations of the Holy Spirit, that He may never be ashamed of us whom He dared to love and counsel against the great day of judgment; through Jesus Christ our Lord, with You and the Father, one God, with dominion over us forever. Amen.

The Hymn concluded   Author unknown
                                                        Italian Hymn

Come, Holy Ghost, in love
(Selected stanzas)

Interlude

Countdown to Pentecost (IV)
Gifts of the Holy Spirit, Isaiah 11:2

Might

Many Hebrew words can be translated "might" (or "strength" or "power"). God is "all-mighty," omnipotent. In the New Testament the term "powers" carries the idea of the "holders of power," whether people or spirits, rulers or magistrates "the powers that be," Romans 13:1 KJV). In either situation the gift of might from the Spirit to the Branch of Jesse is an exciting gift. Elsewhere (9:6 KJV) Isaiah enumerates the names by which "Child" should be called. Among them is "the mighty God"! He who healed diseases, stilled storms, and raised the dead is indeed mighty. He who forgives sins is mighty. He who sits on the throne of the Kingdom of Power, Grace, and Glory is indeed mighty. St. Paul points out that we die, rise, and rule together with Christ (Romans 6), so "might" is given us. We are given power over Satan in Christ, thus this gift is given to us. We are given the power of the keys, so this gift is given to us—in Christ. Who shall say that the martyrs facing the hostile powers without flinching were weaklings? Or who shall say that love conquering hatred, subduing anger, or ministering to lepers is weakness?

The Hymn   Heinrich Held
                                        Komm, o komm, du Geist

Come, oh, come, Thou quick'ning Spirit
(Selected stanzas)

The "Might" candle is lit

The Scripture   Galatians 5:22

The Collect

Holy Spirit, Giver of wisdom and understanding, counsel and might, knowledge and fear and piety, we pray that the gifts all be ours, but just now let the gift of might be given us that we by it and in Christ our Lord have strength to face all vicissitudes, all trials and temptations, all challenges to Christian living, and even martyrdom, should it be required of us; through Jesus Christ our Lord, with You and the Father, one God, with dominion over us forever.

The Hymn concluded   Heinrich Held
                                        Komm, o komm, du Geist

Come, oh, come, Thou quick'ning Spirit
(Selected stanzas)

Interlude

Countdown to Pentecost (III)
Gifts of the Holy Spirit, Isaiah 11:2

Knowledge

Knowledge is accumulated facts as known by a person or by mankind. A book of knowledge is a book of assumed truths about a given subject. In the Old Testament, and often implied in the New, knowledge carries the idea of "experiencing good or bad." Reality happens. Knowledge apprehends the reality. God is very real. Knowledge of God implies a recognition of and obedience to Him (Isaiah 43:10). The New Testament often maintains this Old Testament concept for knowledge in phrases such as "to know sin," "to know the truth," "to know Christ."

It is the Old Testament usage of "knowledge" that is the knowledge given by the Spirit. Christ, the Branch of Jesse's root, "knew" God, that is, He experienced Him; He was obedient to Him by the gift and power of the Spirit. It is the Spirit's good pleasure to help us to "know" God. Through Him we learn to call God "Father."

Through Him we affirm Jesus as Lord. Through Him, we are convinced of and rely upon Him, the Comforter, the Paraclete.

The gift of knowledge extended by the Spirit implies also faith and love and hope. It is a great gift, indeed, for in the end it is the gift of eternal life in glory with God.

A Hymn   Joseph Hart
                                        Boylston

Come, Holy Spirit, come!
(Selected stanzas)

The "Knowledge" candle is lit

The Scripture   Matthew 25:14-30

The Collect

Holy Spirit, our Sanctifier, continue to call us, enlighten us, and keep us all in the one true faith, that we, knowing and experiencing our Lord, might produce Your fruits in time to the praise of God and the well-being and peace of our peers; through Jesus Christ our Lord, with You and the Father, one God, with dominion over us forever.

The Hymn concluded   Joseph Hart
                                        Boylston

Come, Holy Spirit, come!
(Selected stanzas)

Interlude

Countdown to Pentecost (II)
Gifts of the Holy Spirit, Isaiah 11:2

Fear of God

"The fear of the Lord" dominates both the Old and the New Testaments. In our day this "fear" perhaps ought to be thought of as "awe" or "dread." It is occasioned by man's recognition of God's purity and, in contrast, man's own sinfulness. The gap between God and man is momentous. "Behold," Abraham said, "I have taken upon myself to speak to the Lord, I who am but dust and ashes" (Genesis 18:27). This awe, this fear, is a continuing factor in man's relationship to God through both Testaments. The cross is meaningful only against the background of man's sin and the fury of God's righteous wrath. God's love, which seems the dominating message of the New Covenant, is nonetheless controlled by the concept of His purity.

Jesus received the "fear of God" as a gift of the Spirit. He was made to be sin for us, and so understood the gap sin occasions between man and God far better than we. "Awe" and "dread" indeed accompanied Him into the depths explored and experienced on the cross.

We dare never speak of the "love of God" without the awareness of the great gulf between our Lord and us. As children have both "fear" and "love" for their fathers, so we Christians have "fear and love" of our heavenly Father.

A Hymn   Martin Luther
                                                       Nun bitten wir

We now implore God the Holy Ghost
(Selected stanzas)

The "Fear of God" candle is lit

The Scripture   1 John 4:18-21

The Collect

Holy Spirit, who witnessed our creation with excitement, who saw our fall with dismay, and who intercedes for us with groaning, keep us aware of the transcendent purity of the Father that we may always be aware in our sinfulness of our unworthiness, that we may stand in constant dread and awe of Him, and that we may be the more deeply grateful for His abiding love in Jesus Christ; through the same Jesus Christ our Lord, with You and the Father, one God, with dominion over us forever. Amen.

The Hymn concluded   Martin Luther
                                                       Nun bitten wir

We now implore God the Holy Ghost
(Selected stanzas)

Interlude

Countdown to Pentecost (I)
Gifts of the Holy Spirit, Isaiah 11:3

Piety

Last but not least, in the list of the gifts of the Holy Spirit is "piety." Since the term "fear of the Lord" occurred twice in the Isaiah list, the translators of the Septuagint (from Hebrew into Greek)

exercised an option and translated the Hebrew once directly as "fear of the Lord" and once as "piety." Through the centuries the church has used "piety" as one of the gifts and in word and symbol has spoken of the seven gifts of the Spirit.

The term "piety" literally means "dutiful conduct toward God (the brother, the nation)." Jesus' life is marked by such obedience. At the age of twelve He was "about His Father's business" in the temple where His distraught parents finally remembered to look for Him. His "decision" in the wilderness for the cross, His determination to go to Jerusalem, His passive resistance to His captors—all emerge from His "piety," a truly noble gift from the Spirit to the Stem of Jesse.

The Spirit gives us no less in Christ. We pray our special prayer, "Thy will be done." We affirm our allegiance and obedience in the faith expressed in the Creeds. We search the Word for the will of God that we might please Him who first loved us, all as we allow the gift of piety to permeate our being.

The Hymn   Michael Schirmer
                                                       Wie schoen leuchtet

O Holy Spirit, enter in
(Selected stanza)

The "Piety" candle is lit

The Scripture   Isaiah 11:2-3

The Collect

Holy Spirit, Giver of all such gifts as sustain our souls and establish and strengthen our covenant relation with the Father, be generous with Your gift of piety, whereby our conduct to the Father may be impeccable and our obedience to Him be unassailable, that our lives, humbly lived, may be beacon lights to lead our peers to Him; through Jesus Christ our Lord, with You and the Father, one God, with dominion over us forever. Amen.

The Hymn concluded   Michael Schirmer
                                                       Wie schoen leuchtet

O Holy Spirit, enter in
(Selected stanza)

A Pentecost Service

Anticipating the Service—a Note

The rhythm of the church year, especially through the festival half, climaxes in Pentecost. In graceful arches Christmas moves into Epiphany. Epiphany arches into the Transfiguration. The talk between Christ and Moses and Elijah at the Transfiguration was about His decease at Jerusalem, thus climaxing the Epiphany season and beginning the thrust of the next arch to the commemoration of Christ's death and resurrection. Easter arches over into Pentecost. Here in the Pentecost explosion the church of Jesus Christ was born and commissioned. From here until the slower rhythm (Festival—nonfestival seasons) works itself out and the feast of Christ the King is celebrated, the church will concern herself in a broad way with the life that issues from the review of the mighty acts of God in Christ through which we have just passed.

Worship this morning incorporates the rhythm of the Easter-Pentecost arch by using an Easter hymn for processional. The general theme for the service is based on an ancient prayer of the church, simple, yet heavy with import. Two psalms have been used, both traditional to Pentecost for reasons suggested in the text. The gifts of the Spirit, enumerated in Isaiah 11:2-3, having been explored in the "Countdown to Pentecost" interludes and symbolized by the seven candles, give way in this liturgy to the fruits of the Spirit mentioned by Paul in Galatians 5:22. Finally the congregation prays, "Maranatha" ("Our Lord, come!" 1 Corinthians 16:22), the continuing prayer of Christ's people. The Benediction is the Lord's blessing on the time between now and His return.

Martin Luther expressed the work of the Holy Spirit in a choice set of words in his explanation to the Third Article of the Apostles' Creed: "Called . . . by the Gospel, enlightened . . . with His gifts, sanctified and kept . . . in the one true faith"! Our worship this morning hopefully allows the Holy Spirit to do just that.

Pentecost

The Order of Worship

The Prelude

The Prayer (Announcement of the theme)

> *Officiant:* "Come, Holy Spirit, fill the hearts of the faithful and kindle in them the fire of Your love"
> *People:* Amen.

(The Lighting of the "Piety" Candle)

The Processional — Thomas Kelly
Neander

Who is this that comes from Edom

The Psalm with the Lesser Gloria (responsively) — Psalm 47

(A psalm celebrating the dominion of God over all gods and over all nations. It is reminiscent of the distant sound of Pentecost's mighty winds.)

The Preparation for the Spirit's Coming
Confession and Absolution

> *Officiant:* Let us confess our unworthiness to God our Father.
> *People:* Cleanse my heart, oh, my Lord. Purge my soul in forgiveness, for I am altogether unworthy of Your love and totally undeserving of Your promises. I am not worthy that You should make this sinful clay Your dwelling place. By the sacrifice of Jesus Christ who was made to be sin for me, purify my heart. Clothe me in Christ's righteousness by faith and trust. Sanctify me to be the temple of the Holy Spirit.
> *Officiant:* In the name of Christ our Lord I exercise the Office of the Keys given to us by Christ and entrusted to me by this community. Be of good cheer. Your sins are forgiven in the name of the Father, of the Son, and of the Holy Spirit.
> *People:* Oh, give thanks unto the Lord, for His steadfast love endures forever.

The Anthem

Part I: "Come, Holy Ghost . . . ."

The Scripture — John 14:23-31

The Hymn — Martin Luther
Komm, Heiliger Geist, Herre Gott

Come, Holy Ghost, God and Lord!
(Stanza 1)

The Scripture — Acts 2:1-11

The Prayer

> *Officiant:* Let us pray:
> *People:* Come, Holy Spirit, fill our hearts; through Jesus Christ our Lord. Amen.

The Hymn   Martin Luther
Komm, Heiliger Geist, Herre Gott

Thou holy Light, Guide Divine
(Stanza 2)

Part II: " . . . fill the hearts of the faithful"

The Scripture   Galatians 5:16-25

The Renunciation and Commitment

Officiant: You having heard the Word of the Holy Spirit as communicated to us through St. Paul, His servant, I ask you, Do you believe that you are the temple of God and that the Spirit of God dwells in you?
People: I do.
Officiant: Do you renounce the works of the flesh?
People: I do renounce them.
Officiant: What works of the flesh do you renounce?
People: I renounce immorality, impurity, licentiousness, idolatry, sorcery, enmity, strife, jealousy, anger, selfishness, dissension, party spirit, envy, drunkenness, carousing, and the like.
Officiant: Do you desire to bring forth the fruits of the Holy Spirit?
People: I do so desire.
Officiant: Which are such fruits of the Spirit toward which you aspire?
People: I aspire toward love, joy, peace, patience, kindness, goodness, faithfulness, gentleness, self-control, as the Holy Spirit fills my heart and life.
Officiant: Let us pray:
People: Come, Holy Spirit, fill the hearts of the faithful and kindle in them the fire of Your love. Amen.

The Hymn   Martin Luther
Komm, Heiliger Geist, Herre Gott

Thou holy Fire, Comfort true
(Stanze 3)

The Sermon

The Votum

The Offering

The Prayers

(Here may follow the celebration of the Eucharist, Baptisms, or the Rite of Confirmation.)

The Pentecost Psalm with the Lesser Gloria   Psalm 67

(Psalm 67 was written and first sung at the return of the Ark of the Covenant to Jerusalem and Zion. From Zion Yahweh, God of the Covenant, extended His dominion over the entire world. Now Christ and His church exercise such sovereignty.)

The Prayer

Officiant: Let us pray:
People: Maranatha; come, Lord! Amen

The Benediction

The Recessional   Thomas Cotterill
Erfurt

Let songs of praises fill the sky

Primer Thoughts for Pentecost

The events and implications of Pentecost lay open any number of possible developments for a service. The event is documented in detail in the "Book of the Holy Ghost." It was an auspicious beginning for the new people of God. Ideas born of grasping the significance of the Pentecost event can readily be forged into exciting liturgy.
1. Miracle upon miracle: Winds, flames, tongues, conversions, baptisms!
2. Done with care, the birthday of the church can be dramatized, her growth celebrated, her health examined, her "cure" restated.
3. A celebration in praise of the Holy Spirit, Soul of the church, Comforter, Teacher.
4. The indwelling Spirit. (A suggestion for Ascension Day concerning the indwelling Godhead might readily be used on Pentecost.)
5. The tower of Babel and the resultant confusion and division contrasted by the centrality of Christ inaugurated at Pentecost and the unifying and barrier-defying "language of love" (agape).
6. Christ's prayer, "Father, forgiven them . . . ," which has protected His church for 19 centuries.

REFORMATION

Notes on the Reformation
A Reformation Service
Primer Thoughts for Reformation

Notes on the Reformation

Perhaps it would be wise to use the Mass from Luther's time to celebrate the Reformation. But the very freedom born in the Lutheran Reformation makes possible free Orders. Here is an Order designed to celebrate the rediscovery of the Gospel.

This service is broken into parts that celebrate the great victory won by Christ, lost or mislaid in the medieval church, and restored in the work of the Reformer. Absolution is a victory over confession; the church ought to celebrate that! The Good News is a victory over the damning Law; Christians ought to celebrate that! The Word is a triumph over Satan; the saints in time and eternity celebrate that! The Reformation of the 16th century was exceedingly good to the church of the 20th.

Pennons, triangular-shaped banners, were a medieval symbol of triumph and victory. Made of "slippery" material, adorned with an heraldic cross, mounted on a 10-foot pole, and carried in processional and in the service, they would add color, movement, excitement, and a real sense of celebration to the service here following. Each time the order calls for "Celebration" the pennons could be carried through the aisle during the celebration of the "victory." The more pennons, the greater the drama (and the involvement). Lacking pennons, banners or ribbons on poles could be used.

A Reformation Service

A Footnote to the Service

Worship is man's response to God. In its broadest sense it is the Christian life. In its narrow sense it is the specific way in which man responds in rites and rituals.

We can worship in various ways. It is sheer excitement for some to worship in the old forms. The centuries have honed and polished the "old forms" until they fairly glisten. It is equally exciting for others to worship in new forms. Such worship is happening experimentally throughout Christendom.

Lutherans are sometimes said to worship with their heads. Lutherans are learning to worship with their other senses as well. Several "devices" are used in this order to bring that about.

There is "drama" in this service. This is not new; the mass is high drama. But the type of drama here is different. There is also light and color and motion, designed to symbolize and stimulate. We hope that the sense of celebration is heightened and that a sense of triumph is realized.

Finally, it perhaps should be added that this style of worship has been chosen since the congregation does not have an order common to all. A "free" order makes possible total participation.

Glossary

Celebrate: to commemorate, to make known, to glorify, to honor, to praise.
Pennon: a long triangular or swallow-tailed streamer typically attached to the head of a lance or ensign; a flag of any shape; a symbol of victory and triumph.
Dialog: (a) a conversation between two or more persons; (b) an exchange of ideas and opinions.

For whatever is born of God overcomes the world; and this is the victory that overcomes the world, our faith. (1 John 5:4)

The Order of Worship

The Organ Prelude

The Preface to Worship

Voices from Centuries Past[1]

Voice 1: In the name of the Father, of the Son, and of the Holy Spirit.

(Pause)

Voice 2: This is the lament of the ages, the unending cry of the human family;

[1] Suggestion: spoken from back of church or over PA system, with microphones hidden.

Voice 3: Kyrie, eleison—Lord, have mercy on us—Kyrie, Kyrie.

Voice 2: And in the fullness of time, the cry of the family of man, the patience of the family of man, was answered. God acted.

Voice 4: "And it came to pass in those days . . . that she brought forth her first-born Son, and wrapped Him in swaddling clothes and laid Him in a manger."

Voice 2: He grew and died and rose again . . . and hope was born in the family.

The Spirit came and the church was born.

And the church grew and became strong, sometimes in favor with God; more often in favor with man!

So the struggle . . . in the fourth century to establish the deity of Christ . . .

Voice 5: We "believe in one Lord, Jesus Christ, the only begotten Son of God, begotten of His Father before all worlds, God of God, Light of Light, Very God of Very God, Begotten, not made, Being of one substance with the Father, By whom all things were made."

Voice 2: So the struggle, in the fifth century to identify the Holy Trinity, and to establish the personhood of the Holy Spirit.

Voice 3: And the catholic faith is this, that we worship one God in Trinity and Trinity in Unity, Neither confounding the Persons nor dividing the Substance. For there is one Person of the Father, another of the Son, and another of the Holy Ghost. But the Godhead of the Father, of the Son, and of the Holy Ghost is all one; the glory equal, the majesty coeternal . . ."

Voice 2: Through the centuries the struggle persists. In the sixth century:

Voice 1: The monasteries with their pious monks.

Voice 2: In the eighth century:

Voice 3: Broken idols.

Voice 2: In the twelfth:

Voice 4: The Crusades.

Voice 2: The fifteenth:

Voice 3: Failing councils

Voice 2: The sixteenth:

Voice 6: "Since then Your Majesty and your lordships desire a simple reply, I will answer without horns and without teeth. Unless I am convicted by Scripture and plain reason—I do not accept the authority of popes and councils, for they have contradicted each other—my conscience is captive to the Word of God. I cannot and I will not recant anything, for to go against conscience is neither right nor safe. Here I stand, I cannot do otherwise. God help me. Amen."

Voice 2: The nineteenth century:

Voice 5: Onward, then, ye faithful, Join our happy throng, Blend with our your voices In the triumph song: Glory, laud, and honor Unto Christ, the King; This thro' countless ages Men and angels sing. Onward, Christian soldiers, Marching as to war, With the cross of Jesus Going on before.

Voice 2: The twentieth century:

(Begin service)

The Processional

Matthew Bridges

Diademata

Crown Him with many crowns
(Stanzas as required)

The First Part

In Christ, Victory Over Sin

A. The Confession

(Psalm 51:1-4 NEB, with thoughts from Matthew 6:9-13)

V. Be gracious to me, O God, in Thy true love:

R. in the fullness of Thy mercy blot out my misdeeds.

V. Wash away all my guilt:

R. and cleanse me from my sin. I have not always hallowed Thy name, nor done the work of an evangelist, nor bent willing to Thy will, nor been a faithful steward, nor forgiven my brother as I have been forgiven, nor avoided temptation and evil.

V. For well I know my misdeeds:

R. and my sins confront me all the day long.

V. Against Thee, Thee only, I have sinned:

R. and done what displeases Thee.

(Silence)

B. The Absolution

V. God shows His love for us, in that while we were yet sinners, Christ died for us. The mercy of God is from everlasting to everlasting. I declare unto you, who have sincerely repented, in the name of Jesus Christ, you are forgiven.

C. The Celebration   Edward Perronet
                                                 Coronation

All hail the pow'r of Jesus' name!
(Choose stanzas)

The Second Part

In Christ, the Victory of Righteousness

A. The Tower Discovery of Martin Luther[2]

The concept "God's righteousness" was repulsive to me, as I was accustomed to interpret it according to scholastic philosophy, namely, as the "formal or active" righteousness, in which God proves Himself righteous in that He punishes the sinner as an unrighteous person . . . until, after days and nights of wrestling with the problem, God finally took pity on me, so that I was able to comprehend the inner connection between the two expressions, "The righteousness of God is revealed in the Gospel" and "The just shall live by faith."

Then I began to comprehend the "righteousness of God" through which the righteous are saved by God's grace, namely, through faith; that the "righteousness of God" which is revealed through the Gospel was to be understood in a passive sense in which God through mercy justifies man by faith, as it is written, "The just shall live by faith." Now I felt exactly as though I had been born again, and I believed that I had entered Paradise through widely opened doors. . . .

As violently as I had formerly hated the expression "righteousness of God," so I was now as violently compelled to embrace the new conception of grace and, thus, for me, the expression of the Apostle really opened the Gates of Paradise.

B. Dialog: Natural Man and The Word[3]

Leader (Natural Man): [Sarcastically] Do you trust entirely in the mercy of God—in Jesus Christ?
"There is a way which seems right to a man . . . ." (Proverbs 14:12)
People (The Word): He said, "I came not to call the righteous, but sinners." (Matthew 9:13)
Leader: "Look, Your disciples are doing what is not lawful to do on the sabbath." (Matthew 12:2)

[2] Ernest G. Schwiebert, *Luther and His Times* (St. Louis: Concordia Publishing House, 1950), p. 286.

[3] Leader (Natural Man) may speak over PA system, from the rear, or from some hidden place.

People: He said, " . . . the Son of Man is Lord of the sabbath." (Matthew 12:8)
Leader: " . . . 'Lo, here it is!' or 'There!' . . . ." (Luke 17:21)
People: He said, "The Kingdom of God is in the midst of you!" (Luke 17:21)
Leader: " . . . 'His blood be on us and on our children!'" (Matthew 27:25)
People: He said, "Father, forgive them; for they know not what they do." (Luke 23:34)
Leader: " . . . 'I thank Thee that I am not like other men . . . .'" (Luke 18:11)
People: "We hold that a man is justified by faith apart from works of law." (Romans 3:28)
Leader: "You are severed from Christ, you who would be justified by the Law; you have fallen away from grace." (Galatians 5:4)
People: " . . . it is by grace, it is no longer on the basis of works; otherwise grace would no longer be grace." (Romans 11:6)
Leader: "For I do not do the good I want, but the evil I do not want is what I do. . . . Wretched man that I am! Who will deliver me from this body of death?" (Romans 7:19, 24)
People: "He died for all, that those who live might live no longer for themselves but for Him who for their sake died and was raised." (2 Corinthians 5:15)
Leader: Do you trust entirely in the mercy of God in Jesus Christ?
People: (Affirmation) I do so trust!

C. The Celebration   A Joyous Anthem

The Third Part

In Christ, the Victory of Gospel over Law
(The Old Covenant vs. the New)

A. The Law   Exodus 20:1-17

B. The Transition   Galatians 4:1-7

C. The Gospel   2 Corinthians 5:18-21

D. The Celebration[4]   Dignus est Agnus

Leader: Worthy is the Lamb that was slain to receive power and riches and wisdom:
People: and strength and honor and glory and blessing.

[4] Done with a fanfare between each versicle.

Leader: Blessing and honor and glory and power be unto Him that sitteth upon the throne:

People: and unto the Lamb forever and ever. (Revelation 5:12-13 KJV)

Leader: Great and marvelous are Thy works, Lord God Almighty:

People: just and true are Thy ways, Thou King of saints.

Leader: Who shall not fear Thee, O Lord, and glorify Thy name?:

People: for Thou only art holy.

Leader: Praise our God, all ye His servants:

People: and ye that fear Him, both small and great.

Leader: Alleluia! for the Lord God Omnipotent reigneth:

People: Alleluia, alleluia! Amen.

The Fourth Part

In Christ, the Triumph of the Word

A. The Office Hymn   Martin Luther
Nun freut euch

Dear Christians, one and all, rejoice

B. The Sermon

Interlude

In Christ, Praise and Thanksgiving

A. The Offering

B. The Anthem   The Choir

C. The Prayers

The Fifth Part

In Christ, the Victory Over Satan

A. Dialog: Satan and Christ

Leader: Do you renounce the devil and all his works, and all his ways?

People: I do so renounce them.

Leader: "The Lord said to Satan, 'Whence have you come?' Satan answered the Lord, 'From going to and fro on the earth, and from walking up and down on it.'" (Job 1:7)

People: "And the angel said to them 'Be not afraid; . . . for to you is born this day in the city of David a Savior, who is Christ the Lord.'" (Luke 2:10-11)

Leader: "And Jesus asked him, 'What is your name?' He replied, 'My name is Legion; for we are many.'" (Mark 5:9)

People: . . . "And the unclean spirits came out, and entered the swine; and the herd, numbering about two thousand, rushed down the steep bank into the sea, and were drowned in the sea." (Mark 5:13)

Leader: "Again, the devil took Him to a very high mountain, and showed Him all the kingdoms of the world and the glory of them; and he said to Him, 'All these I will give You, if You will fall down and worship me.'" (Matthew 4:8-9)

People: "Then Jesus said to him, 'Begone, Satan! for it is written, "You shall worship the Lord your God and Him only shall you serve."'" (Matthew 4:10)

Leader: "Then Satan entered into Judas called Iscariot, who was of the number of the twelve; he went away and conferred with the chief priests and officers how he might betray Him to them." (Luke 22:3-4)

People: "Remember how He told you . . . that the Son of Man must be delivered into the hands of sinful men, and be crucified, and on the third day rise." (Luke 24:6-7)

Leader: . . . "to keep Satan from gaining the advantage over us; for we are not ignorant of his designs." (2 Corinthians 2:11)

People: "The God of peace will soon crush Satan under your feet. The grace of our Lord Jesus Christ be with you." (Romans 16:20)

Leader: Do you renounce the devil and all his works, and all his ways?

People: I do so renounce him, through Jesus Christ my Lord!

B. The Celebration   Martin Luther
Ein' feste Burg

A mighty Fortress is our God

The Sixth Part

Through Christ, Taking the Victory to the World

A. The Benediction

B. The Recessional   William W. How
Gott sei Dank

Soldiers of the Cross, arise

Primer Thoughts for Reformation

Capitalizing on the *Sola Scripture* Reformation principle, out of which the *Fidei* and *Gratia* principles emerge, one might devise a Reformation service based on the concept of the Word of God, especially as the concept is used in Scripture. The service lends itself to the participation of a number of people. Visuals for each part are in order. Here is a viable outline:

The Introduction
    The Word is the mighty acts of God.
        (Here notice could be taken of how at first the Word of God was told and retold until writing was invented and the Word could be written. Psalm 136 speaks to the mighty acts.)

Part the First
    The Word is Scripture.
        (A responsive reading based on 2 Tim. 3:15-16 can be easily worked and fitted here. A brief message expounds the concept.)

Part the Second
    The Word is the incarnate Christ.
        (There are passages that amplify John 1;1 ff., that can be worked into a responsive reading, edifying the worshiper and honoring Christ. The battle hymn of the Reformation fits under this section.)

Part the Third
    The Word is in the mouth of the brother.
        (Why not use quotes from some "brothers" [and "sisters," too]? Brother Martin could speak; Dietrich Bonhoeffer could have a word. Then the brief message from a live brother to cap it.)

Part the Fourth
    The Word is prophetic; the end-time.
        (A word out of Revelation is appropriate, and a hymn from the communion of saints is in order.)

Part the Fifth
    The Word is Law and Gospel.
        (The Law bends men to their knees; the Gospel raises them to full height in Christ. The opportunity for a missionary thrust is wide open.)

Epilog
    Recapitulation.
        (A hymn like "O Word of God Incarnate" has an excellent ability to draw the aforementioned parts into focus. In fact, a sentence prayer might be written to be prayed between stanzas. A closing Collect and the Benediction bring the service to a close.)

THANKSGIVING

A Thanksgiving Day Service
Primer Thoughts for Thanksgiving

Five Kernels of Corn[1]
(A Thanksgiving Tradition)

"'Out of small beginnings great things have been produced, as one small candle may light a thousand.'—Gov. Bradford.

I

"'Twas the year of the famine in Plymouth of old,
The ice and the snow from the thatched roofs had rolled.
Through the warm purple skies steered the geese o'er the seas,
And the woodpeckers tapped in the clocks of the trees;
The boughs on the slopes to the south winds lay bare,
And dreaming of summer the buds swelled in air,
The pale Pilgrims welcomed each reddening morn;
There were left for rations but Five Kernels of Corn.
        Five Kernels of Corn!
        Five Kernels of Corn!
But to Bradford a feast were Five Kernels of Corn!

II

"'Five Kernels of Corn! Five Kernels of Corn!
Ye people be glad for Five Kernels of Corn!'
So Bradford cried out on bleak Burial Hill.
And the thin women stood in their doors white and still.
'Lo the Harbor of Plymouth rolls bright in the spring,
The maples grow red, and the wood robins sing,
The west wind is blowing, and fading the snow,
And the pleasant pines sing, and arbutuses blow.
        Five Kernels of Corn!
        Five Kernels of Corn!
To each one be give Five Kernels of Corn!'

[1] Hezekiah Butterworth in *Holy-Days and Holidays*, compiled by Edward M. Deems (New York and London: Funk & Wagnalls, 1902), pp. 373—74.

III

"O Bradford of Austerfield, haste, on thy way
The west winds are blowing o'er Provincetown Bay,
The white avens bloom, but the pine domes are chill,
And new graves have furrowed Precisioners' Hill!
'Give thanks all ye people, the warm skies have come,
The hilltops are sunny, and green grows the holm,
And the trumpets of winds, and the white March is gone,
And ye still have left you Five Kernels of Corn.
            Five Kernels of Corn!
            Five Kernels of Corn!
Ye have for Thanksgiving Five Kernels of Corn!'

IV

"'The raven's gift eat and be humble and pray,
A new light is breaking, and Truth leads your way.
One taper a thousand shall kindle: rejoice
That to you has been given the wilderness voice!'
O Bradford of Austerfield, daring the wave,
And safe through the sounding blasts leading the brave,
Of deeds such as thine was the free nation born,
And the festal world sings the 'Five Kernels of Corn.'
            Five Kernels of Corn!
            Five Kernels of Corn!
The nation gives thanks for the Five Kernels of Corn!
To the Thanksgiving Feast bring Five Kernels of Corn!"

Preservice Thoughts

Five Kernels of Corn . . .

Preparation for this Thanksgiving service turned up the poem on the cover. The last line of it was intriguing enough to borrow for a framework for this service. The line is a refrain within the service, a constant reminder that by comparison to almost all people of history and probably most people living today, Americans are blessed out of measure. In one sense, thanksgiving ought to happen without horizontal glances, for to look over and "up" could cause jealousy; to look over and "down" could spoil the day. Yet, one ought to keep in mind that many people's thanksgiving is for "five kernels of corn," and against our corn patch, that is not very much. Rejoice and thank the Giver of all gifts for the good gifts you enjoy, quietly mindful of the "five kernel" people with whom we can better share having counted our own.

A Thanksgiving Day Service

"Carlyle has somewhere said, that a man should put himself at zero, and then reckon every degree ascending from that point an occasion for thanks. Precisely on this scale do the Scriptures compute our mercies."—Wm. Adams

The Order of Worship

The Prelude

The Processional   Author unknown
                                         Kremser

We praise Thee, O God, our Redeemer, Creator

A Collect for the Presence of God

Holy Spirit, who moves the hearts of Your people to praise and thanksgiving, since we are come together into this place of worship to offer gratitude and glory for God's endless gifts to us, we bid Your presence among us, together with the presence of our Lord Jesus Christ, and of the heavenly Father who created and still preserves us, one Lord, our God, world without end. Amen.

A Responsive Reading   (Psalm 148 TJB)

Pastor: Let heaven praise Yahweh:
      praise Him heavenly heights,
People: praise Him, all His angels,
      praise Him, all His armies!
Pastor: Praise Him, sun and moon,
      praise Him, shining stars,
People: praise Him, highest heavens,
      and waters above the heavens!
Pastor: Let them all praise the name of Yahweh,
      at whose command they were created;
People: He has fixed them in their place for ever,
      by an unalterable statute.
Pastor: Let earth praise Yahweh:
      sea-monsters and all the deeps,
      fire and hail, snow and mist,
      gales that obey His decree,
      mountains and hills,
      orchards and forests,
      wild animals and farm animals,
      snakes and birds,

all kings on earth and nations,
princes, all rulers in the world,
young men and girls,
old people, and children too!
People: Let them all praise the name of Yahweh,
for His name and no other is sublime,
transcending earth and heaven in majesty,
Pastor: raising the fortunes of His people,
to the praises of the devout,
of Israel, the people dear to Him.

The Gloria Patri

Five Kernels of Corn!
Five Kernels of Corn!
To the Thanksgiving Feast bring Five Kernels of Corn!

I

God of Our Fathers

The Hymn   Daniel C. Roberts
National Hymn

God of our fathers, whose almighty hand
(Stanzas 1—3)

A Scripture   (Ecclesiasticus 44:1-4; 8-9a; 10-15 TJB)

Pastor: Next let us praise illustrious men, our ancestors in their
successive generations.
People: The Lord has created an abundance of glory, and displayed
His greatness from earliest times.
Pastor: Some wielded authority as kings and were renowned for
their strength; others were intelligent advisers and uttered
prophetic oracles.
Others directed the people by their advice, by their
understanding of the popular mind, and by the wise words of
their teaching; . . .
People: Some of them left a name behind them, so that their
praises are still sung.
Pastor: While others have left no memory, and disappeared as
though they had not existed.
People: But here is a list of generous men whose good words have
not been forgotten.
In their descendants there remains a rich inheritance born
of them.

Their descendants stand by the covenants and, thanks to
them, so do their children's children.
Their offspring will last for ever, their glory will not fade.
Pastor: Their bodies have been buried in peace, and their name
lives on for all generations.
The peoples will proclaim their wisdom, the assembly will
celebrate their praises.

The Hymn concluded   Daniel C. Roberts
National Hymn

Refresh Thy people on their toilsome way
(Stanza 4)

The Message

A Collect of Thanks for Our Forefathers

Lord Jesus Christ, Ruler of the affairs of mankind, for the fearful
people who settled our land when it was new and who established the
principles by which we still seek to govern ourselves, we tender thanks
to You, and pray for fearless men and women who will continue to
contend for our way of life under God and the kind of freedom that
implies; who with the Father and the Spirit, are one God, living and
reigning, world without end. Amen.

Five Kernels of Corn!
Five Kernels of Corn!
To the Thanksgiving Feast bring Five Kernels of Corn!

II

God of Creation and Preservation

The Hymn   John S. B. Monsell
Wie lieblich ist

Sing to the Lord of harvest

The Message

A Collect for the Seedtime and Harvest

Lord the the seedtime and harvest, who set all living things in
motion and who maintains them in constant care, we are grateful for
the life-sustaining gifts which we receive from Your hand each day,
praying that there be always enough to supply the needs of the whole
human family until the end of time, through Jesus Christ, who with
You and the Spirit, are one, eternal God. Amen.

Five Kernels of Corn!
Five Kernels of Corn!
To the Thanksgiving Feast bring Five Kernels of Corn!

III

God of History

The Hymn   Samuel F. Smith
America

My country, 'tis of thee
(2 or 3 stanzas)

A Continuing Call to Prayer   (The Gettysburg Address)

Fourscore and seven years ago our fathers brought forth on this continent a new nation conceived in liberty, and dedicated to the proposition that all men are created equal.

Now we are engaged in a great civil war, testing whether that nation, or any nation so conceived and so dedicated, can long endure. We are met on a great battlefield of that war. We have come to dedicate a portion of that field as a final resting-place for those who here gave their lives that that nation might live. It is altogether fitting and proper that we should do this.

But, in a larger sense, we can not dedicate—we can not consecrate—we can not hallow—this ground. The brave men, living and dead, who struggled here, have consecrated it far above our poor power to add or detract. The world will little note, nor long remember what we say here, but it can never forget what they did here. It is for us the living rather to be dedicated here to the unfinished work which they who fought here have thus far so nobly advanced. It is rather for us to be here dedicated to the great task remaining before us—that from these honored dead we take increased devotion to that cause for which they gave the last full measure of devotion; that we here highly resolve that these dead shall not have died in vain; that this nation, under God, shall have a new birth of freedom; and that government of the people, by the people, for the people, shall not perish from the earth.

The Hymn concluded   Samuel F. Smith
America

Our fathers' God, to thee
(Last stanza)

A Scripture   (Isaiah 2:2-4)

Pastor: It shall come to pass in the latter days that the mountain of the house of the Lord shall be established as the highest of the mountains,
People: and shall be raised above the hills; and all the nations shall flow to it,
Pastor: and many peoples shall come, and say:
People: "Come, let us go up to the mountain of the Lord, to the house of the God of Jacob; that He may teach us His ways and that we may walk in His paths."
Pastor: For out of Zion shall go forth the law, and the word of the Lord from Jerusalem.
People: He shall judge between the nations, and shall decide for many peoples;
Pastor: and they shall beat their swords into plowshares, and their spears into pruning hooks;
People: nation shall not lift up sword against nation, neither shall they learn war any more.

Five Kernels of Corn!
Five Kernels of Corn!
To the Thanksgiving Feast bring Five Kernels of Corn!

IV

God of All Mankind

An Anthem

The Message

A Collect for All People

God of all gods, Lord of all people, who by virtue of creation holds dominion over all of us, maintain and sustain the hearts of all who know and acknowledge You as Lord, break open and claim the hearts of all who follow other gods; and in Your patience, love, and power grant us all Your continual benediction; through Jesus Christ, our Lord, who with You and the Spirit reign forever. Amen.

The Thanksgiving Offering

Five Kernels of Corn!
Five Kernels of Corn!
To the Thanksgiving Feast bring Five Kernels of Corn!

V
God of the Future

The Meditation

The Hymn   Matthaeus A. von Loewenstern
                                            Herzliebster Jesu

Lord of our life and God of our salvation

A Collect for the Future

Lord of time, God of eternity, whose divine plan is fixed and whose timetable is rigid, we pray that judgment against the world be stayed until many, many more be prepared to say their thanksgivings before Your throne; through the Holy Spirit, through whom the Gospel of Christ is spread, who reign and rules with You, O Father, and with You, O holy and beloved Son. Amen.

The Benediction

The Recessional   St. Francis of Assisi
                                            Lasst Uns Erfreuen

All creatures of our God and King

Primer Thoughts for Thanksgiving

1. Through the prophet Isaiah the Lord bids the Israelites look to the rock whence they were hewn and to the pit whence they were dug, to Abraham their father and to Sarah who bore them. Americans with their short history need a memory, too. Thanksgiving offers opportunity to remember and reflect, to pray and praise. Such a service using memory and praise might outline something like this:

I. Memory and Remembering
   The long memory—Psalm 136
   The long memory for us—The Mayflower Compact
   A somewhat shorter memory—
      The first National Proclamation
      of Thanksgiving by George Washington.

II. Cognition and Recognition
   Proclamation of Thanksgiving Day—
      for the current year.

III. Pray, praise, and give thanks.

2. The Thanksgiving Order may recall and embellish the sweeping movement of God toward us and our response to Him. "The cattle on a thousand hills" are God's. Redemption in Jesus Christ and sanctification through the Holy Spirit are of God. All that we are and have and hope to be we owe to our heavenly Father. An order raising to visibility the great gifts of God, balanced with the response of praise and thanks, and issuing in obedience to the holy will of God, might work out like this:

Introduction: Establishing our relationship with God anew:
   Confession and Absolution
   1. Our God has acted for us.
      A proper hymn
      A fitting sermon
   2. The Sacrifices
      a. Of praise
         Using a Psalm (67)
         A praise hymn
         With prayer
      b. Of thanksgiving
         With Scripture
         (say, Deut. 26:1-12 or Luke 17:11-19)
         With a song of thanksgiving
         And a prayer
      c. The service of obedience
         The Apostles' Creed
         The Offering
         A Hymn of Consecration
   3. From God's house to God's World
      A Collect
      The Benediction

AN ALTERNATIVE TO THE MASS

Notes
A Worship Service

Notes on an Alternative to the Mass

The Mass has its own unique outline as it moves through the history of salvation to total commitment. Anyone not interested in the message for the day is nonetheless exposed to Christ in each of its liturgical actions.

If the Mass is to be replaced, something similar ought to be offered. An alternative service should, of itself, aid the worshiper as it exposes him to the great, sweeping movement of God. Here is a fumbling example. It is based on the "soldier" metaphor used by St. Paul and the vocation theology developed by Luther.

Christians are people holding the parapets or marching forth to battle for King Christ. All week they are at their battle stations. They are battered by the world and bruised by their own consciences. On the Lord's Day they are given time for rest and recuperation. The healing processes are applied to them at the outset; then the orders to again "go forth" are given. The soldiers disperse to their assigned positions for another week.

The service is done with hymns in place of sung liturgy. It is quite possible to draw liturgical propers from contemporary sources (e.g., Contemporary 2)* and insert them into the service. The sermon, coming at the end, has the strong motivation built in by the Eucharist to its advantage and, while it must be Gospel-oriented, gives opportunity to stress the Christian life without being legalistic.

Note Before the Service

This service sees the *laos* (people of God) as an army, with every man at his assigned place. The soldiers of Christ are returned for the moment to the gathering place for rest and recuperation. They are

*Contemporary Worship, 2, *Services, The Holy Communion,* The Inter-Lutheran Commission on Worship, The Lutheran Church—Missouri Synod and others, 1970,

healed through the touch of Christ in the Sacrament and through the holy Gospel. Healed and rested they are returned to their posts on the battlements, where they do battle with evil again, and again seek to "wrest" souls from perdition.

The Order of Worship

The Prelude

The Processional Hymn   William Hammond
                                                                    Vienna

Lord, we come before Thee now

The Trinitarian Invocation   (Password to the Community)

Pastor: Thank our Lord for His enduring love and for the marvelous things He has done for us.

People: Praise and thanksgiving be to the everlasting Father and to His Son, who has redeemed us through the shedding of His blood, and to the Holy Spirit, Guarantor of our eternal heritage with Christ, the Lord of glory.

The Confession and Absolution (Examination of returning soldiers)

Pastor: Let us confess in deep humility and to our shame that we have by our unworthy thoughts, our unthinking words, and our self-centered deeds offended the triune God who loves us with steadfast and enduring love.

People: (Symptoms)

(*Will confess silently, privately, before the throne of the Holy One, then . . .*)

                                                                    (Cauterizing)

Pastor: O God,

People: Gracious God, I have sinned and forfeited my right to be called Your child. I am sick at heart, for I have dared to offend You; I am astonished and ashamed that I have shown so little concern for my fellowman. I beg Your forgiveness yet again, O gracious God. Be merciful to me, and for Jesus' sake forgive me.

                                                                    (Cleansing)

Pastor: In the name of God, our Lord, I announce forgiveness to each of you who has honestly confessed his sins, earnestly repented of them, and sincerely accepted Christ as Savior and Lord.

The Hymn   (Praise on Being Cleansed)
                                Edward Perronet
                                Coronation

All hail the power of Jesus' name!
(Stanza 1)

The Consecration   (Preparation for Healing)

The Distribution   (Ministry of the Great Physician)

A Distribution Hymn

The Post-Communion Praise   (The Healing Is Complete)

A Hymn   Philipp Nicolai
                                Wie Schoen leuchtet

How lovely shines the Morning Star!
(Stanza 6)

The Prayer   (An Expression of Gratitude)

Pastor: Let us pray.
People: Praise and thanksgiving are Your right, beloved Father, for renewing for us our sainthood in Jesus Christ and for a new opportunity to serve You in Your kingdom and to show our love for You by living in love.

(A Further Expression of Gratitude)

Have mercy on all impenitent souls and hold rebellious mankind in Your steadfast love. Be with those among us, eternal Father, whose burdens in these days are heavy and whose sickness brings them pain and misery. Guard those among us who are young, and watch carefully those who are old, that the young may be living testimonies of the faith, and the old may live victoriously in the faith. Keep our community of saints vibrant and alive in Christ, our Lord, and grant blessing to the whole Christian church on earth. Amen.

The Good News According to: (For Renewed Strength)

The Office Hymn

The Message   (Inspiration)

The Prayers   (Commitment)

The Gospel (or Epistle)   (Marching Orders)

The Hymn   (Orders Reiterated)

The Nicene Creed   (Raising the Standard)

The Benediction   (Blessing the "Troops")

The Recessional Hymn   (Dispersion to Posts)

The Silent Worship

70

A NARRATIVE COMMUNION SERVICE

Notes
A Narrative Communion Service
Primer Thoughts for Narrative Communions

Notes on a Narrative Communion Service Based on the "Mass"

A "narrative" service is one that explains the ongoing movement of the liturgy. Explanatory comments are interspersed with the action. The narrator stands to one side of the chancel and as unobtrusively as possible reads his commentary. The officiant pauses for the narration, then continues with the action. In some narrative services, the comments may occur in the middle of a thought. A service such as this is an excellent educational tool.

A Narrative Communion Service

Notes on the Service

God is recognized where He has broken through to invade human history. His invasion has always been for the welfare of mankind. Climactic in the God-events is indeed the "Word made flesh to dwell among us," that we might behold the glory of God. No event in all history exceeds the life, death, and resurrection of Jesus our Lord.

The church, faced with the necessity of ordering its formal response to the divine invasion, built the church year to remember God's great acts. But a year is a long time, and the church bridged the time factor with a weekly remembrance. Eventually even the day was broken into the seven canonical hours, in which the suffering, death and glory hour of Christ were rehearsed. Finally, in the Order of Holy Communion, in a single hour, the whole sweeping panoramic history of salvation was caught and held. The worshiper is bid remember step by step the fall of the first parents and the first promise, the birth, life, suffering, death, resurrection, and ascension of Jesus.

As we worship now, notice and remember how Jesus is kept in sharp focus from beginning to end. You will not be allowed for a single moment to forget Him. Our worship once again becomes an experience with God. It is an involvement, an encounter with the Redeemer.

The Order of Worship

An Opening Hymn of Praise

Narrator: This order is for Holy Communion. The format has evolved through the centuries of the church's past. It has been a malleable format, changeable with the times, yet enduring through those times. The Order is educational; it retells the story of our Lord's purpose for His coming, His passion, His death, and His resurrection. It is great worship; it brings the Christ of history into focus and calls Him into an existential presence. It is majestic; in stately manner it proclaims Jesus, the risen Christ, Lord and King.

Further, the Order of Holy Communion (as must be with any service) is a healing Order. The sinner, returning from the world to the gathering of the faithful, brings his bruised and battered self to be touched with the nail-torn hand of the forgiving Christ. Healing takes place. Wholeness comes again. Nor should one forget to add that a service with Holy Communion is a special impelling force for God's man. Healed, rested, restored, filled, he marches forth to live his life for his Lord.

This is a "narrative Communion." As narrator, I will try to interpret what is happening as the service progresses.

An Invocation

A Call to Repentance and Absolution

Narrator: The recital begins in the Garden of Eden, where man, in Adam, fell from grace and became "a poor, miserable sinner." As sinner he is under God's judgment and condemnation. We are all Adam's children by nature. But we have been made Christ's family by Baptism and faith. At the outset, we are reminded by revisiting Eden, with its judgment and its promise, whence we came, and by whom we have come, in the Confession of Sins and Absolution.

The Confession and Absolution

The Introit and Gloria Patri

Narrator: Through the long reaches of history men waited and yearned, prayer and hoped for the appearing of God's mercy in Jesus Christ.

The Kyrie

Narrator: And then God acted! The announcement to the world was made first to Palestinian shepherds. Suddenly it is Christmas again and we are caught up into an echo and amplification of the song of the angel hosts.

The Gloria in Excelsis

The Collect for the Day

Narrator: Jesus grew and waxed strong in wisdom and stature and in favor with God and man. Then, when the time was right, and God's hour for Christ was at hand, John the Baptist appeared at Jordan's banks, and called people to repentance, that the way might be prepared for the Messiah.

The Epistle

Narrator: Then Christ appeared to begin His public ministry. "Repent, the kingdom of God is at hand," He cried. Out of His God-origins He put mighty content into stories He saw in His human situation, and men learned to know God anew—and aright. From His power to forgive sins and His burning desire that men be made whole, people walked and heard and breathed again. The proud were recalled from their high places, and the lowly and the sinner found hope. Ah, the wonder of the holy ministry of Jesus.

The Gospel

The Nicene Creed

The Office Hymn

The Sermon

Narrator: The great pendulum of God's clock swung near to the hour of Christ's glory. Like flint He set His face to go to Jerusalem to drink the cup of suffering.

The Offertory

The Offering

The Prayers

Narrator: We move fast now into Holy Week and stand at the side of history to watch the pageant pass. We are caught up in the memory of how He went from death to life for us. As the liturgy unfolds, we relive our own death and rising to new life in Him. And, seeing Him in His servanthood, we, too, are impelled to the servant role.

The Sursum Corda

The Eucharistic Prayer, through the proper Preface

Narrator: Our Lord arrived in Jerusalem, riding in triumphant procession. Jerusalem's people gathered in the streets to chant His praise. We are caught for the moment in the memory of the original event, but even as we chant the ancient song, our hearts soar upward to the reigning King.

The Eucharistic Prayer, concluded

The Sanctus

The Lord's Prayer

Narrator: Monday passed, and Tuesday. Wednesday came and ended with the setting sun. On Thursday He commandeered a room to celebrate the Passover. They gathered as the sun moved toward the horizon. He washed their feet. He led them in discussion. He prayed for them. And then,

The Consecration

The Pax

Narrator: They arrested Him. They led Him bound to Caiaphas. They took Him to Pilate for sanction to murder Him. The forces of heaven aligned against Him as judgment against the sins of the world was concentrated in Him. Satan mocked with hellish glee. It was Friday, the day of our Lord's death by condemnation, but the day of our deliverance.

The Agnus Dei

Narrator: He died. They laid Him in the cave. They sealed the opening with a huge stone. Then Easter. "He is not here! He is risen as He said!" To Mary, He said: Peace. To the disciples His word was: Peace. To Thomas the word was: Peace.

In Word and sacrament, but uniquely in the Sacrament, He comes still, to each of us who comes, and the Word in the bread and wine, the body and blood, is yet the same: Peace! Peace! Peace!

The Distribution

Narrator: When forty days had passed and He had showed Himself alive to many people He took them to a mountain for His ascension. He disappeared from their midst. His work as Redeemer was finished. In glory, He sits at the right hand of the Father, ruling in majesty over the three great Kingdoms—of Power, Grace, and Glory—in which we hold citizenship.

On the mountaintop He gave His command to evangelize the world, and to teach His people all things that He had commanded. His promises were there for all going forth in obedience: "I have all power in heaven and in earth. I am with you."

So we "depart in peace," with the reassurance of our salvation, which is ours to carry to all people, for we are lights to the unbelieving world and to those who need to see God in His mercy, lest they perish forever.

The Nunc Dimittis

The Thanksgiving

The Benediction

Primer Thoughts for Narrative Communions

It is possible to do a variety of services with running commentaries, for there are a variety of ways of hearing the traditional orders.

1. The various parts of the service can be introduced with passages from Scripture. For instance, the traditional Trinitarian Invocation might be introduced with Exodus 20:24: "In all places where I record My name I will come unto thee, and I will bless thee." One caution is in order. It is easy to become too wordy.

2. The service can be treated academically, with each part analyzed and its presence in its position accounted for. A certain deadliness creeps into such a presentation. Naming the various parts of the service is more a classroom activity than a worship experience.

3. Starting with baptism, the service can become an amplification of the whole concept of baptism. The "dying and living with Christ" are present in the Confession/Absolution; nourishing the baptized occurs in the Office of the Word; the Eucharist confirms the baptismal covenant and the community, and realigns those who commune with the goals and purposes to which they were set at their Baptism.

4. God is a "sending God." The Christian community is involved in the mission, the *missio Dei*. When a man worships, prays, or thanks, he declares himself on God's side and therefore on God's mission. Worship and mission ought not to be separated. Worship as response happens all week; mission happens all week. When we worship we are in mission; when we are in mission, we are worshiping. It becomes a truth that worship impells us to be in mission. The Invocation reminds us that we are under the dominion of the "sending God." The Word supplies our motive and direction. Prayer declares us on the side of the "sending God." The Creed is the "banner" under which we travel. The Song of Simeon is our declaration of readiness to die for Christ in the world.

5. There are other "undercurrents" in any worship hour. As the utilities supply service to the homes in the city, so the separate parts of the liturgy supply living Water, the Light of the world—the day's message from God.

6. Narrative accompaniment may be adapted to all the rites and ceremonies of the church. Why not work out a wedding narration and include it in a service in which marriage is theme? It is possible to develop a narration for a Baptism or installation of officers. Matins and Vespers and other services also lend themselves to comment, although it is difficult to discover continuity in the orders themselves.

AN ORDINATION AND/OR INSTALLATION SERVICE

Notes
A Service of Ordination and of Installation

Notes on an Ordination and/or Installation Service

Ordinations and installations are going on all the time, for the visible church is fluid. Not only its members, but its pastors move about. As the elderly pastors step aside, new and eager young pastors take up the challenge of the Kingdom. As missions are established, young and active pastors are set to the task of building. For each new pastor there is an ordination to the call. For each pastor making a change there is an installation. The brethren in the ministry and the calling people gather in worship to lay on hands and to bless and pray for the person and the work of the ordained.

Here is an ordination/installation service. Through Word and prayer God's presence and purpose is announced. The ordinand (or installee) boldly announces his baptism, in fear and trembling he declares his dedication, in joy and promise he is set to the task. In this order some of the words of installation/ordination are Lutheran. Others may readily be substituted. The brethren promise to uphold him and those with whom he will work join hands in yoke-fellowship with him. An order printed out in its entirety, hymns, psalm, questions and answers, help to draw the worshiping congregation deep into the commitment of their pastor.

A Service of Ordination and of Installation

Notes to Help You Understand This Service

This service divides into four parts. Each centers on a crucial aspect of what we are doing as a young man stands up to be counted for Jesus Christ and kneels in commitment to Jesus Christ. This is the hour of his ordination into the ministry of Jesus Christ, and his installation as a pastor for Jesus Christ.

The first part sets our Lord before the community, invoking Him through psalms, songs, Scripture, and the Word in the heart of a brother.

Part two establishes the fact that we are all members of the body of Christ, ordained by our baptisms to the priesthood, and branded (sealed) by it to Jesus Christ. The ordinand here attests to his baptism.

What has been tacit in other ordinations is made explicit in the third division. The call is into the kingdom of God, the holy Christian church, the communion of saints, for it is the Holy Spirit in its midst who calls. The profoundest moment in this hour is the commitment by a young man to the Kingdom and to martyrdom for it, should his history require it.

Finally, the immediate vocation required of the ordinand is as _____ in _____ Congregation. Here the long traditions of the church are practiced, from his declaration of conviction to the laying on of hands by the brethren, a practice indeed as old as the church.

Let it be said that the worship centers in our Lord Christ, not in the ordinand, and that we are all involved in the worship quite as much as he.

Service of Ordination
into the Ministry of Jesus Christ
and of Installation
as _____
at
_____ Church
of
_____

The Prelude

The Processional

Part One

Praise and Exhortation

The Hymn of Invocation   Martin Luther
Komm, Heiliger Geist, Herre Gott

Come, Holy Ghost, God and Lord!

The Psalmody with Gloria   Psalm 148
(A Cosmic Hymn of Praise)

The Anthem

The Prayer

The Office Hymn   Author unknown
                                                                 St. Agnes

O Jesus, King most wonderful

The Meditation

A Little Time for Reflection

Part Two

Baptism and the Community

The Hymn   Johann J. Rambach
                                                           O dass ich tausend

Baptized into Thy name most holy

The Lection with Responses   Romans 6:3-11 (The Jerusalem Bible)

Lector: "You have been taught that when we were baptised in Christ Jesus we were baptised in His death";

People: In my baptism I died with Christ.

Lector: "in other words, when we were baptised we went into the tomb with Him and joined Him in death,"

People: At my baptism I was buried with Christ.

Lector: "so that as Christ was raised from the dead by the Father's glory, we too might live a new life."

People: Through my baptism I was raised with Christ.

Lector: "If in union with Christ we have imitated His death, we shall also imitate Him in His resurrection. We must realise that our former selves have been crucified with Him to destroy this sinful body and to free us from the slavery of sin."

People: By my baptism I died and rose again with Christ.

Lector: "When a man dies, of course, he has finished with sin. But we believe that having died with Christ we shall return to life with Him: Christ, as we know, having been raised from the dead will never die again. Death has no power over Him any more. When He died, He died, once for all, to sin, so His life now is life with God; and in that way, you too must consider yourselves to be dead to sin but alive for God in Christ Jesus."

People: Through my baptism I live for Christ.

(Scripture selections from here to end of Part 2 from TJB)

Officiant: "Unless a man is born from above, he cannot see the kingdom of God." (John 3:3)

People: "All baptised in Christ, you have all clothed yourselves in Christ." (Galatians 3:27)

Officiant: "Just as a human body, though it is made up of many parts, is a single unit because all these parts, though many, make one body, so it is with Christ." (1 Corinthians 12:12)

People: "In the one Spirit we were all baptised." (1 Corinthians 12:13)

Officiant: "You are a chosen race, a royal priesthood, a consecrated nation, a people set apart to sing the praises of God" (1 Peter 2:9)

People: "who called you out of the darkness into His wonderful light." (1 Peter 2:9)*

Officiant: "Remember it is God Himself who assures us all, and you, of our standing in Christ, and has anointed us, marking us with His seal and giving us the pledge, the Spirit, that we carry in our hearts." (2 Corinthians 1:2-22)

People: Glory to be the Father and to the Son and to the Holy Ghost; as it was in the beginning, is now, and ever shall be, world without end. Amen.

Pastor: _____ , have you been baptized in the name of the triune God?

Ordinand: Yes, I have been baptized in the holy name of God the Father, God the Son, and God the Holy Spirit.

Pastor: Lead us then in the confession of the holy Christian faith into which we have been baptized, as it is expressed in the Apostles' Creed.

All: I believe in God the Father Almighty, Maker of heaven and earth.

   And in Jesus Christ, His only Son, our Lord; who was conceived by the Holy Ghost, born of the Virgin Mary; suffered under Pontius Pilate, was crucified, dead, and buried; He descended into hell; the third day He rose again from the dead; He ascended into heaven and sitteth on the right hand of God the Father Almighty; from thence He shall come to judge the quick and the dead.

   I believe in the Holy Ghost; the holy Christian church, the communion of saints; the forgiveness of sins; the resurrection of the body; and the life everlasting. Amen.

*"Enlightenment," "out of darkness," in the New Testament as in patristic writers, always refers to Baptism.

Part Three

The Call and the Kingdom

The Hymn   Johann E. Schmidt
Fahre fort

Zion, rise, Zion, rise
(Stanza 1)

The Scripture   Matthew 10:16-20, 24-27

The Hymn   Johann E. Schmidt
Fahre fort

Bear the cross, bear the cross
(Stanzas 2 and 3)

The Scripture   1 Timothy 6:11-16

The Hymn   Johann E. Schmidt
Fahre fort

Run thy race, run thy race
(Stanza 4)

The Affirmation of the Call to the Kingdom

Officiant: Since the days of Pentecost the holy Christian church, the communion of saints, has extended from Jerusalem to include people from all the reaches of the world. The Holy Spirit has been faithful to His charge. By your baptism you were initiated into the holy Christian church. You have been sustained by the power and purpose of the Holy Spirit in the one true faith in Jesus Christ. The prayers and love of your parents, your sponsors, and of the Christian community have supported you. You present yourself before us this day for ordination (or installation) into the holy ministry.

I therefore ask you, do you believe that you have been called by the Holy Spirit to serve the living God as a minister for Jesus Christ?

Ordinand: I do so believe.

Officiant: Have you answered God's call to be a minister for Jesus Christ?

Ordinand: I have said "Yes" to my Lord Jesus Christ.

Officiant: Are you ready to follow the commands of Jesus Christ? He said, "Go into all the world to preach the Gospel." Are you prepared to go where He wills?

Ordinand: I have said "Yes" to my Lord Jesus Christ.

Officiant: Jesus said, when He had washed the disciples' feet, "I have given you an example." Are you prepared to minister to the least of humanity if He so wills that for you?

Ordinand: I have said "Yes" to my Lord Jesus Christ.

Officiant: Jesus said, "Thou shalt love the Lord thy God and thou shalt love thy neighbor as thyself." Are you prepared to love your neighbor as yourself?

Ordinand: I have said "Yes" to my Lord Jesus Christ.

Officiant: Jesus said, "Feed My sheep and feed My lambs." Are you prepared to nourish His people with the milk and meat of the Word?

Ordinand: I have said "Yes" to my Lord Jesus Christ.

Officiant: Jesus said, "Blessed are you when men revile you and persecute you for My name's sake." Are you prepared to suffer all, even martyrdom, for the sake of the Kingdom?

Ordinand: I have said "Yes" to my Lord Jesus Christ. May He keep me faithful to the end.

Officiant: _____ , in the name and stead of God the Father, God the Son, and God the Holy Spirit I publicly confirm your call by the Holy Spirit to serve as herald and minister in Christ's holy church and to the whole family of man. May the Heavenly Preserver protect you, the Holy Comforter renew you, and the Eternal Redeemer fill your heart. May God give you a full measure of all the Christian virtues, of wisdom, and of courage to do His work.

Now in the name of the blessed Trinity I consecrate you a minister in the body of Christ and send you forth to do the will of Christ, who is Head over all things to the church. May the grace of our Lord Jesus Christ, the love of God the Father, and the communion of the Holy Spirit be and always abide with you. Amen.

The Anthem   "Jesus, Who Didst Ever Love Me"
Johann Sebastian Bach

Jesus, who didst ever love me,
Jesus, who didst set me free,
Jesus, here I stand before Thee,
Jesus, take me unto Thee.
Jesus, do not ever leave me.
Jesus, do Thou e'er befriend me.
Jesus will guide my endeavor,
Jesus will be at my side;
Jesus will protect me ever,
Jesus will with me abide.
Jesus will great strength me render,
Jesus will be my Defender.

The Prayer

Part Four

Ordination and Installation

The Hymn   Edward Osler

Kommt her zu mir

Lord of the Church, we humbly pray

The Ordination to the Ministry at _____ Congregation

Ordinator: Dearly beloved brother, Our Lord and Savior Jesus Christ said unto His disciples: "Go therefore and make disciples of all nations, baptizing them in the name of the Father and of the Son and of the Holy Spirit, teaching them to observe all that I have commanded you; and lo, I am with you always, to the close of the age."

"When He ascended on high He led a host of captives, and He gave gifts to men. . . . And His gifts were that some should be apostles, some prophets, some evangelists, some pastors and teachers to equip the saints for the work of ministry, for building up the body of Christ."

Whereas, after due training, you have been found well versed in Christian doctrine and able to teach others and have been called to the office of the holy ministry in this congregation,

And whereas, dear brother, you have accepted the call extended to you by this congregation and are about to enter upon the duties pertaining to the holy office of the ministry, in accordance with the Word and the will of the Lord Most High, I now ask you in the presence of God and this congregation:

Do you believe and accept the canonical books of the Old and New Testaments to be the inspired Word of God and the only infallible rule of faith and practice?

Ordinand: I do so believe.

Ordinator: Do you accept the three Ecumenical Creeds—the Apostles', the Nicene, and the Athanasian—as faithful testimonies to the truth of the Holy Scriptures and do you reject all the errors which they condemn?

Ordinand: I do.

Ordinator: Do you believe that the Unaltered Augsburg Confession is a true exposition of the Word of God and a correct exhibition of the doctrine of the Evangelical Lutheran Church; and that the Apology of the Augsburg Confession,

the two Catechisms of Martin Luther, the Smalcald Articles, and the Formula of Concord—as contained in *The Book of Concord*—are also in agreement with this one Scriptural faith?

Ordinand: I do.

Ordinator: Do you solemnly promise that you will perform the duties of your office in accordance with these Confessions and that all your teaching and your administration of the sacraments shall be in conformity with the Holy Scriptures and with the aforementioned Confessions?

Ordinand: I do.

Ordinator: Will you, finally, adorn the doctrine of our Savior with a holy life and conversation?

Ordinand: I will, the Lord helping me through the power and grace of His Holy Spirit.

_____

Officiant: Members of _____ Church Council, elected representatives of the community of Christ which calls itself _____ Congregation, you have heard _____ attest to his holy baptism, through which he was initiated into the body of Christ, you have heard him publicly affirm his allegiance to Jesus Christ, Head over all things to the church, and his readiness even for martyrdom for the cause of Jesus Christ. You have heard him further declare his subservience to the Holy Scriptures and his adherence to *The Book of Concord*. You are witnesses to his declaration that he will, God helping him, seek to be an example of Christian living.

Will you confirm the call which the congregation extended to _____ ? Will you work with him to build the kingdom of Jesus Christ, to edify the members of the body of Christ in this place, and will you honor and uphold him in the office to which in this very hour he has committed himself?

Council: We will.

_____

Officiant: Brother members of the office of the holy ministry, you have heard the witness of _____ to the Christ who is your Lord and Master, to the Holy Scriptures which you uphold, and to *The Book of Concord* to which you are sworn in your office of the ministry of the Lutheran Church. Will you accept him as your brother, uphold him in the faith, comfort and strengthen him in his need with the holy Word, and bear him in your prayers to the throne of the Most High?

The Brethren: We will.

_____

Ordinator: I now commit you to the holy office of the Word and the sacraments. I ordain you a minister of the church and install you as _____ of this congregation in the name of the Father and of the Son and of the Holy Spirit. May the Lord pour out on you His Holy Spirit for the office and work committed to you by the call of this congregation, that you may be a faithful dispenser of the means of grace and servant to God's people. Amen.

(The Assisting Ministers lay on hands and speak an appropriate benediction over him.)

The Prayer (all praying)

Holy Spirit, Lord of the church, who has always distributed gifts for the edifying of the saints and who has appointed some to be pastors in the flock of the Great Shepherd, use the gifts You have given to this Your servant, now ordained pastor, to proclaim the Word of repentance and peace to sinful people, to speak the Word of comfort and hope to the fearful and the dying, and to live the Word as a beacon light to the flock and all the world, for the sake of the kingdom of Jesus Christ, our Lord. Amen.

The Lord's Prayer

Ordinator: Go, then, exercise your concern over all the flock over which the Holy Spirit has made you shepherd, to feed the church which He has purchased with His own blood. Feed the sheep and lambs; be an example to the flock. And when the Chief Shepherd shall appear, may you receive a crown of glory. The Lord bless you from on high and make you a blessing to many, that you may bring forth fruit to the glory of the Chief Shepherd and Bishop of your soul. Amen.

The Anthem
Based on Psalms 5:8 and 4:8
Samuel S. Wesley

Lead me, Lord, lead me in Thy righteousness

The Pastor: The Collect for the Church
The Collect for Peace
The Benediction

The Recessional Hymn
William J. Danker
Mission or Sine Nomine

The sending, Lord, springs from Thy yearning heart